Living Mysteries

A Practical Handbook
for the Independent Priest

the apocryphile press
BERKELEY, CA
www.apocryphile.org

apocryphile press
BERKELEY, CA

Apocryphile Press
1700 Shattuck Ave #81
Berkeley, CA 94709
www.apocryphile.org

Cover photo of the private oratory of Rev. William Myers used by permission.

DEDICATION

Dedicated to Elizabeth Schaaf, for good cooking, and to Matt Lippa for good questions.

With thanks to Mark Whitehead, Josephine Dunne, Deborah DeLong, Ron Wood, Catherine Adams, Tony Hash, Larry Terry, Grace Franco, Alberto LaCava, Jim Rule, Lynda Martin, Jessika Lucas, Tim Harris, Josephine Shaffer, Richard Shaffer, Paul Blighton, Ruth Blighton, Marian Linda Carter, Will Cameron, Basil Wilby, Violet Firth, Will Myers, Rob Angus Jones, Rosamonde Miller, Sarah King, Mary Ray, Jo Foy, David Spell, Linda Beaman, Sciencia Fleury, David Goddard, Phillip Burmeister, John Michael Greer, Sara Greer, David Kling, Mario Schoenmaker, Kristina Kaine, Jeff Ingle, Joan Ingle, John Morgan, Harry Vedder, Katherine Kurtz, and especially to Tim Kaltenbach. You are all priests forever, after the order of Melchizedek.

BY THE SAME AUTHOR

*The Many Paths of the
Independent Sacramental Movement*

Who Are the Independent Catholics?
(with John R. Mabry)

CONTENTS

Notes on the Meditations 8

Meditation: An Invitation 11

Chapter One: Priesthood...13

Chapter Two: The Sacraments 21

Chapter Three: The Spiritual Life 69

Chapter Four: Chapel and Equipment 88

Chapter Five: Cycles of Prayer................................96

Chapter Six: Training..113

Chapter Seven: Conclusion 132

QUOTATIONS

I don't want disciples—I don't want any part of it. All I want to do is to put a torch in their hands and open the door. If they want to run through, fine. If they don't, fine; but I don't want any disciples.

—*Rev. Frida Waterhouse, interview in Bismullah, Summer 1978, 14-16*

Did you know that there was a time that I had a preaching roster? Anyone who was a priest could preach. The church very slowly became empty and I suddenly realized that our priests cannot preach... woeful, terrible, some of them shouldn't be allowed outside their own front doors. So I changed it. Only those priests that I knew had the ability to speak could preach. The upheaval was incredible—after all, they were ordained to preach! No, no, they were not ordained to preach, they were ordained to do what God wants them to do. They are not ordained to perform liturgy. Some people never get it. Liturgy means that you are a good dramatist. The psychodrama people will do nicely, although they may bugger it up wanting to do their own thing. They may want to stand on the altar. You have to perform a play on the altar, and some people can't do that, no matter what. They have lead feet—wherever they tread, everything collapses. You can't teach them liturgy or ceremony as you can't teach them to act in a play. Then they wonder why they are ordained. They are ordained because of the Melchizedek Priesthood, not necessarily in order to preach. They need a heart that opens and flows in a certain direction, a direction that God has implanted in their hearts. That is all there is to it. Can you understand that?

—Rev. Mario Schoenmaker, Deliberations on St Mark (Victoria, Australia: Independent Church of Australia, 1984, Chapter 55, p.5.)

As generous distributors of God's manifold grace, put your gifts at the service of one another, each in the measure he has received. The one who speaks is to deliver God's message. The one who serves is to do it with the strength provided by God. Thus, in all of you God is to be glorified through Jesus Christ.

—1 Peter 4:10-11a

Note on the Meditations

Scattered throughout this book, there are a number of visual meditations. This form of visionary inner work was popularized in western Christianity by the *Spiritual Exercises of St Ignatius of Loyola*, the founder of the Jesuits. I first learned this kind of meditation from a Jesuit priest, Father W. Norris Clarke. Working inwardly with these mysteries has strengthened my priesthood and my contact with the spiritual realities I am called to mediate. These meditations have proven useful to others, and I hope they will be helpful to you, as well.

To do the meditations, you simply sit comfortably in a chair, on a stool, or on the floor, with your back relatively straight. As the late Zen teacher Jiyu-Kennett Roshi liked to say, meditation posture should make you feel normal, not strange! You may light a candle or incense if you wish. Let your body, mind, and emotions become calm and balanced. Make a simple invocation for divine protection and guidance, such as the sign of the cross. If you are new to meditation, you may want to make a recording of the meditation text, or have someone read it to you. If you are more experienced, you may just familiarize yourself with the content, and then allow it to unfold inwardly. In either case, it is appropriate for the meditation to change as you do it. The workings were written down as they appeared in my imagination, and they may shift in your experience. I make no claims for historical accuracy or theological purity in these visions. I can only say that they arise directly from my own experience, and I am convinced that the graced imagination has the potential to be an organ of spiritual perception. Dion Fortune suggested that, during meditation, one should allow things to unfold naturally, acting as if the inner experience is literally true. Engaging the critical faculties mid-vision is a sure method for short-circuiting spiritual experience. However, at a later moment, it is important to examine our experiences in light of all knowledge available to us. When the meditation is finished, make a closing gesture (e.g., the sign of the cross), and be sure you have returned to full outer awareness. If need be, get up and move around, or have something to eat or drink. You may also want to make notes. As with dreams, visionary experience often fades quickly, if not recorded.

Doing a meditation repeatedly over a period of at least one to two weeks will usually prove more fruitful than only doing it once. Some people find visualization easy, while others will engage primarily through another sense, such as hearing or feeling. These are simply individual differences. You will quickly find which your strongest inner senses are. If a felt-sense comes easily to you, but visualization does not, you should work with the feeling, and not worry about the strength of the visualization. For more on visionary meditation from an esoteric perspective, I recommend *Patterns in Magical Christianity* and *Contacting Spiritual Beings* by Nicholas Whitehead, *Magical Images and the Magical Imagination* by Gareth Knight, and *The Magical Training of the Initiate* by Josephine Dunne. A more mainstream Christian perspective can be found in *The Other Side of Silence* by Morton Kelsey.

An Invitation

I invite you to lay aside all cares, and sink deep into meditation for a few moments, resting in God's presence....

We are walking down a stony street, trying to remember the directions we have been given, looking for a house where Jesus and his friends are dining tonight. The evening is drawing on, and we start to wonder if we've taken a wrong turn. But then we notice an unusual collection of people entering a house just past an upcoming curve in the street.

There is a soldier of the conquering Roman Army, a woman who looks for all the world like a prostitute, and an elderly religious scholar. There are a few others, too. We can't see them well in this light, but they look none too clean or respectable. However, we have come a long way, hunger is gnawing at our stomachs, and we might as well see what this most strange teacher is about.

With a bit of nervousness, we walk up to the door, and knock thrice upon it. As the door opens, we see that it is Jesus himself who has opened it for us. He stands before us, framed in the flickering light from inside. He takes our hands in his, greeting us warmly. Jesus draws us into the room, where his friends are gathered about a simple table

11

set with bread and wine. Their gentle eyes meet ours, and we know we shall never hunger or thirst again....

CHAPTER ONE:
The Priesthood

Every human being is already a priest, in a very primal sense. We stand between earth and sky, like pillars in an ever-moving temple. We find ourselves within and among other humans and many other orders of being (stones, plants, animals, elementals, angels, etc.) with energies flowing back and forth, consciously and not. Those of us who are parents mediate the entry of another being into fleshly existence. (For this reason, Mary might be rightly considered the first Christian priest, as the one who literally birthed Jesus.) Our outer personalities mediate the sacred presence at the core of our being, more or less well. We are all points in an extraordinarily complex web, through which divine power moves. That power, the energy of the Holy Spirit, is much greater than us, and not particularly concerned about whether we understand how it is working, at any given moment.

Some forms of Protestant Christianity have given us the notion of being our own priest. While this idea that I am my own priest, needing no other, certainly does appear in Reformation thought, there is another, less known and more profound perspective. At times, we find the teaching that you are my priest, and I am your priest, each person mediating to others and receiving in turn. In our ecological age, with a heightened sense of the interdependence of life, we are well situated to deepen our sense of connection, and our awareness of the spiritual energies which flow among us. We are all, in Lloyd Meeker's happy words, extensions of divine action to one another. Or, as Sciencia Fleury put it, what is priesthood but walking around reflecting God back and forth to one another?

The innate priesthood of the human being always exists and is always available, without further elaboration. However, it also forms itself into streams or inner bloodlines which flow through history. These streams or lineages each mediate a particular mystery, and carry certain specific work through time and space. Belonging to a particular priesthood lineage does not make one better, more spiritual, or more connected than any other being, human or otherwise. It simply means that the work of that spiritual stream is part of one's own work in life. Priesthood lineages are not unlike biological families. One inherits genetic strengths and weaknesses from one's family, as well as positive and negative influences from childhood. Likewise, an inner stream also carries both positive and negative aspects which have built up over the centuries, as well as the more immediate influence of your teachers and initiators. "Our flesh is as the flesh of our brethren, and our children as their children." (*Nehemiah* 5:5) A wise priest learns to work with the negative part of her inheritance (for instance,

Christianity's tendency to make itself the exclusive cus-
todian of truth, and to limit the role of women), striv-
ing to bring it into balance, as much as possible, in her
own life.

No matter how much we may think we have made a
choice to be ordained in a tradition, it is the tradition
which chooses us. Circumstances arrange themselves as
needed, and consecrating grace descends on our heads.
Our only real choice is whether we cooperate, or fight
against it. God can use the most unlikely people,
including us. Depending on our individual calling, we
may work with, and be ordained in more than one tradition, but once consecrated in a lineage we cannot
turn our back on it. If we try, it will come knocking,
louder and louder, until we re-open the door. We also
have a responsibility to carry the lineage forward. We
cannot simply preserve it untarnished like a pretty esoteric museum piece. Rather, we have to feed it from our
own substance, letting it grow through us, and then
hand it forward to those who come after us, whoever
they may be. To fail to transmit what we have received
is to dam a stream until it becomes a stagnant pond
rather than free-flowing, clear water.

The foundational stream which lies behind much of
the western esoteric tradition is the mysterious "priesthood after the order of Melchizedek," the reality of
which is not likely to be found in the array of contem-
porary organizations bearing the name. We could enter
into the contested realm of Biblical scholarship regard-
ing the original meanings of this phrase in scripture.
But perhaps it is best to simply acknowledge that, for
centuries, western esotericism has posited an inner

stream of priesthood flowing back to the mysterious figure of Melchizedek, the priest-king who visited Abraham, and shared bread and wine with him.

Melchizedek is said to be without father and mother. He is not born, he does not die. He is of the timeless realm of the Divine. He is the point where God sacrifices the state of Ultimate Being to step into human flesh, and share a meal with us. In this light, is it any wonder that the epistle to the Hebrews says that Jesus of Nazareth is of Melchizedek's priesthood?

If you are working with, or contemplating the possibility of working with, any stream of priesthood in the western esoteric traditions (Hermetic, Pagan, Christian, or otherwise) it can be fruitful to attempt contact with the being of Melchizedek, however understood. You can simply light a candle, with bread and wine laid out before it. Going into vision, beyond the candle, you see the radiant darkness of the Divine beyond all names and forms. Stars begin to appear in the darkness … and from this field of stars steps the timeless Melchizedek. This being is equally likely to appear in female or male form. In my experience, when female, she often takes the form of Black Sarah, the mysterious figure whose rudderless boat appeared from nowhere to guide Mary Magdalene and her company to the shore of France. He appears to you in the way most appropriate to your own spiritual destiny, and his/her guise may reveal much about your own lines of priesthood. Sit and commune with this figure, in silence or in conversation. Share in the bread and wine. When complete, offer thanks to the inner contact who withdraws again beyond the flame. Finally, extinguish the candle. Even if the contact seems vague and without specific content or guidance, be sure to watch carefully for signs following in your outer life, which may bring the needed message or connection. You may also want to repeat the meditation on a regular basis. As long as you work with what you are given, the contact will deepen, and you will be guided to the ways, ordained or not, in which you are called to express priesthood in your life.

The particular lineage on which we will focus in this book is that of the Christ, although one could easily apply the same principles to other transmissions. I have covered the historical background of this lineage in detail in my book, *The Many Paths of the Independent Sacramental Movement*, and refer the reader there for more information. According to legend, Jesus of Nazareth separated and blessed his apostles, giving them authority in the Holy Spirit. The apostles then consecrated bishops, who would be responsible for teaching and the sacramental life of the newly forming churches. The bishops in turn ordained priests, deacons, and minor clergy to assist them in these tasks. The historical reality was almost certainly more messy than this tidy picture of succession. Nonetheless, many churches (Roman, Anglican, Orthodox, Oriental Orthodox, Assyrian, Moravian, some Lutherans, and others) preserve a priesthood in "apostolic succession" or the "historic episcopate" with a hands-on-heads link that runs back into at least the early centuries of the Christian movement. Some other churches (Methodist, for example) have a ministry which also derives from this priesthood, yet with some break or shift in the transmission.

Through some schisms in western churches, augmented by small missions from eastern churches, the apostolic succession passed into an ever-multiplying number of tiny churches, independent of the larger, historic jurisdictions. This was a process which took place over several centuries, coming to something like the current situation by the early 1900s. There have also been a number of claims to bring through a new or renewed priesthood of Christ, through direct inspiration. Many of these new priesthoods have since become conjoined with apostolic succession in the independent sacramental movement. With efforts like l'Eglise Gnostique of Jules Doinel and the Liberal Catholic Church of Charles Leadbeater and James Wedgwood, esoteric perspectives found their way into the independent churches. The result of all the foregoing is the independent sacramental movement: a broad range of communities which share a number of characteristics in common: small communities and/or solitary clergy; experimentation in theology and liturgy; mostly unpaid clergy; ordination available to a large percentage of the membership; a sacramental and Eucharistic spirituality, with a mediatory priesthood, in most cases preserving the historic episcopate.

The twentieth century saw the profusion of these tiny churches, traditional, esoteric, and otherwise, although their size and eccentricity kept them largely below the radar of the cultural mainstream. These early years of the twenty-first century are witnessing this priesthood breaking free of the structured churches, orders, and groups which it has served heretofore. Shortly before his death in 1997, Rev. Mario

Schoenmaker (founder of the Independent Church of Australia) tried to inaugurate a "free priesthood." After Mario's death, this project foundered, although it is undergoing reconsideration in the ICA at the time of this writing, with different opinions about how such a free priesthood would be related (if at all) to the ICA. To my mind, it is high time to take Mario's inspiration and run with it. Church structures are often an impairment to getting anything done, and can be very unwieldy in small communities, to the extent of appearing comic and all but fictional in nature. The priesthood of Christ does not require this level of outer organization. It can simply exist as a person to person spiritual lineage, with cooperation and friendship happening in ad hoc, anarchic ways. All the heavy accretion of titles, degrees, groups, positions, government recognition, and the like can simply fall away. As Caroline Casey once wisely remarked (on her "Visionary Activist" radio program), "Keep the sacraments—toss the church!"

It is primarily for the free priests of Christ, who have tossed their crutches into the wind, that this book is written. These are brave souls, relying on no support beyond the reality of their inner contact, and the efficacy of their spiritual work. They are themselves living mysteries, carrying the future of the Christian tradition in their hands. To them, I offer what I have learned along the way.

MEDITATIONS

I invite you to lay aside all cares, and sink deep into meditation for a few moments, resting in God's presence....

We find ourselves in a small workroom, lit by the soft light of early morning. Outside the window, we see the light reflecting off the white and gold of the nearby temple. A beautiful young woman sits before us, weaving a cloth of red, purple, and blue. She is concentrated on her work, but looks up as the room fills with a sense of pressure. Blue and golden light swirl in a column before the maiden Mary, and a voice sounds, as if from the center of all things, "Hail, Mary..."

The intensity of the archangel's presence is almost too much for us, and we fail to catch much of Mary's conversation with this mighty messenger. But we see the simple beauty of her wonder at the angel's message, and catch our breath as the conversation falls into a moment of waiting silence.

Mary speaks, "Be it done to me according to your word," and we hear a deep chord of joy resound through the whole earth. We feel new life stirring, not only in Mary, but also in our own bodies. Together with the Virgin, we lift our souls in quiet praise....

CHAPTER TWO:

The Sacraments

The sacraments are the church's magic, the rites which effectively link us to the transforming power of Christ, through the use of simple things of earth— water, oil, bread, wine, and human hands. The history and theology of the sacraments make fascinating reading, but our focus in this chapter is different. The following is a simple and straightforward guide to how to actually perform the sacramental rites. By doing, one will gain practical understanding, which will give the grounding needed for further study to make sense on more than an intellectual level.

A newly ordained priest would be wise to work with other, more experienced clergy as much as possible. There is much that has to be 'caught', rather than 'taught', as Rev. Joe Miller used to put it. Also, in this age of spiritual marketing, there should never be any charge for the sacraments. This is grace, freely given. Of course, there is nothing wrong with freely-offered donations, or with (for example) meeting the travel expenses of a priest who flies across the continent to conduct a wedding. But these rites do not come with a price tag. In the immortal words of Rev. Mario Schoenmaker, "God is very cheap!"

Before we consider the specific sacraments, I offer you some general guidelines for the priest, from Father Paul Blighton's book, *The Philosophy of Sacramental Initiation* (San Francisco, CA: Holy Order of MANS, n.d., pp. 21-23), which has been very helpful to me. As this book is not widely available, I will quote at length:

1. First and most important, as we have said, is to clear the mind completely as you enter the sanctuary. Leave all worldly matters behind. Your only tools are your faith and your knowing. With a clear mind and a concentrated devotion and an unwavering knowing you will function as a perfect channel for the grace and power of Christ to flow through you.

2. Develop a love for the sacraments. Study the function of ritual. Learn the art of working at the altar, so that you get a feeling for the fine points of the priestly craft. You are the modern alchemist. The altar is your workbench. The rituals are your tools.

3. Enjoy your work. Don't be afraid to express the joy of working with the Spirit. A pontifical or stiff pious demeanor has no purpose on the altar. Remember the sacraments are real. The Spirit is real. There is no need for any kind of false front to put them across. Some-times you may be full of tears. Let them flow freely. The joy you feel will be felt by the receiver and will help him to achieve a state of acceptance. A joyless priest is a spiritual contradiction.

4. Perform the actions and pronounce the words of the ritual with clarity and feeling. This is not just form. Every action of the ritual has a higher spiritual coun-

terpart—the invisible reality of the Heaven world. It is the responsibility of every priest to learn how to live and function in this Heaven world. Remember you have left the earth. You are no longer tied to its limitations.

5. Don't forget that you are not alone when you are in the sanctuary. There are always others there that you may not see—the Host above. The sacraments are not just for you but are an important part of the cosmic plan for this orb; and the work of the priesthood is linked to the work of the Hierarchy of Heaven. As far as we are concerned this is the White Brotherhood [or, we might say the Communion of Saints]. When working in the sanctuary it is good practice to ask for their help because we may not know all there is to know about the person or situation we're helping. They see from a fuller perspective and will fill in when needed.

6. Always leave room in ritual for the manifestation of the Spirit. If something comes to you strong and true from the Spirit, give it forth. These things are not necessarily for your benefit but for the receiver, and it is your responsibility to see that he gets it. This does not mean that you can put on a personal performance nor does it give you license to tamper with the ritual. The wise priest respects the ritual but is always open to the gifts of the Spirit as they are given.

7. Above all be conscious of one thing, you are the key to all the sacraments. You are the mediator. You in your own being provide the link that unites earth and heaven in the Holy rituals. Cultivate a sense of responsibility to the priesthood. There is no greater honor than to be consecrated in service to the Great Creator.

We are the handmaidens of God. Remember, once ordained, you no longer have a right to a life of your own. Be ever vigilant to maintain a standard of conduct that will always reflect the dignity of our profession, but withal be yourself.

There has been much debate over the number of sacraments over the centuries. Perhaps the resolution of the question doesn't really matter much. Below, we will consider most of the rites which have been considered sacraments by substantial numbers of Christians. In my instructions, I will use fairly traditional language for God. Those who prefer alternative language can easily make adaptations. Also, I will provide a meditation in each section, which can be used to deepen one's inner connection to the energy of the sacrament in question.

Baptism

Baptism is the sacrament of entry to the community of the Christ. One descends into the waters of death, and rises up again, being conformed to the pattern of initiation one finds in the life of Jesus of Nazareth.

Baptism may be administered to a person of any age, from infant to elderly, and can be celebrated by any baptized person. A priest is not necessary. Some traditions even allow for baptism by proxy, in which a living person is baptized on behalf of a dead person. If this is done, it should not be an attempt to force the dead person to accept the baptism, but rather is an offer which can be freely accepted or rejected.

In the case of older children and adults, baptism is generally preceded by a period of learning about and participating in the Christian tradition. Sometimes persons who are going through such a preparation for baptism are welcomed by a formal ritual of being signed with the cross as "catechumens" (from a Greek word meaning "one under instruction"). Depending on the community, the preparation period may be relatively simple, or full of elaborate rituals.

Baptism is only done once in life. It is a permanent link to the purifying and life-giving power of the Christ. But, if there is doubt about whether a candidate might have been baptized already, the once-for-all nature of the sacrament is traditionally acknowledged through using a conditional formula: "If you have not already been baptized, I baptize you...."

As a ritual of death and resurrection, and a sacrament using the purifying power of water, baptism can often start a larger process of purification in the life of the recipient—on physical, mental, emotional, and spiritual levels. One should be prepared for this possibility, and the person administering the baptism should be willing to help support the neophyte in such a process.

The essence of baptism is very simple. The person being baptized (or the parent or guardian, if it is an infant or small child) should be asked if they accept the mystery signified in the sacrament, the dying and rising of Christ. If your community uses a creed, the question could take that form. The ideal would be for the candidate to be plunged naked, three times, under natural flowing water, while the words are spoken: "N____, I baptize you in the name of the Father, and of the Son, and of the Holy Spirit. Amen." Of course, this is not always (or even often) possible, and the simple pouring of a small amount of water over the head is more than sufficient. One might see in vision the water washing through the entirety of the candidate's being.

There are many ways to elaborate the rite. One can bless the water, recalling the rivers flowing from Eden, the story of Noah and the flood, the passage through the Red Sea, and the baptism of Christ by John the Baptist. One might use salt (purification) and oil (spiritual light), and the laying on of hands in blessing. The candidate can be given a new name (such as the name of a saint) representing a new identity linked to the Christian tradition. The candidate may be clothed in white and given a lighted candle.

Baptism may be done at any time, but is traditionally administered on Easter, the day when the Christian community recalls the death and resurrection of Jesus, in which the baptismal candidate participates. If Easter is not possible, finding another festival (such as Epiphany, the Baptism of Christ, or Pentecost) which links to the nature of the rite can be powerful.

Baptism remains a touch-point for the remainder of one's journey on this way. One might place a dish of blessed water by one's door or altar, which one could touch and use in blessing to remember one's baptism. Or one can sprinkle water over those gathered for the Eucharist, as a blessing, purification, and reminder.

In the event that parents do not wish to have their child baptized as an infant, it is still very appropriate to bless the child, dedicating him or her to Christ, with the sign of the cross. The story of Joseph and Mary dedicating the child Jesus at the Jerusalem Temple would be fitting as a reading for the blessing of an infant or small child.

MEDITATIONS

I invite you to lay aside all cares, and sink deep into meditation for a few moments, resting in God's presence... We stand on a rocky hill outside the gate of the city. Although it is spring, there is a strange chill in the air. We can hardly bear to look up, where three men are raised on crosses, being executed by the Roman soldiers who lounge casually below them. The man in the center is our teacher, Jesus, stripped and tortured.

Those gathered below are mostly the curious and the scornful. But we are in a small group of Jesus' close friends. His mother stands by us, and the Magdalene, and the young disciple John. While their grief is surely greater than our own, they place their hands on our shoulders in comfort. We see Mary's silent tears, as she witnesses the painful death of the one who was once her small child, dancing joyfully amidst his playmates.

Jesus speaks from the cross, with difficulty. "I thirst." Someone lifts up a sponge filled with vinegar, which he barely touches with his mouth. Then he cries with all his remaining strength, "It is finished!" bowing his head in final surrender. With this shout, a veil within us seems to rip wide open, and in vision, we see the wounds of the Christ in our own body, his blood flowing from us….

We look up one more time, pondering the mystery of the sign placed by Pilate above Jesus' head, "This is the King…"

Confirmation

Having been purified through the waters of baptism, which carry us deep into the underworld, and back up again, we then are illumined by the light of the Christ, shining down from the sun above, and from the sun within our own being.

As baptism is our sharing in the death and resurrection of Christ, so confirmation is our sharing in the gift of the Holy Spirit at Pentecost.

The traditional form for confirmation is very simple. It is always administered by a priest, and most often by a bishop. As in baptism, a new name can be given, if desire or inspiration dictates. The priest simply takes chrism (blessed oil) and anoints the person, usually on the forehead or crown, but also sometimes on other points of the body, while saying, "N____, be sealed with the Holy Spirit," or similar words. The priest then lays hands on the candidate's head, and prays silently or aloud that the Holy Spirit will descend and illumine the candidate's life. The priest may blow across the candidate's face, or even give them a small slap on the cheek. (The Irish bishop who confirmed me gave me a handshake, and told me the world was my oyster!)

In esoteric orders descended from the work of Paul Blighton, one priest lays hands on the candidate's head, while another places her hands over the front and back of the solar plexus area (the actual center of the body), forming a cross of light within the body. From the center of this cross, the illuminating presence of the Spirit of Christ is called forth.

Confirmation can be administered at any age, even to

infants. Nonetheless, I believe it is best to wait until a person is approaching some degree of conscious spiritual illumination, so that the rite can connect to the grace they are already experiencing, and be of maximum effect and benefit.

Confirmation is really the completion of baptism, and some have considered them two parts of one sacrament. Depending on the circumstances, confirmation can be administered immediately following baptism. Like baptism, it is received only once, and should not be knowingly repeated.

MEDITATIONS

I invite you to lay aside all cares, and sink deep into meditation for a few moments, resting in God's presence....

We are gathered with Jesus' other friends in a simple upper room. Our joy in Jesus' resurrection has become confused. The Lord left us mysteriously, charging us to watch and pray for his gift to us. Fear has begun to creep back in our hearts, and we fret over what may happen to us at the hands of the religious and political authorities.

The light shines through the small windows, and we shift position on the rough wooden floor, as we look around the room. In the center of the room sits Mary, the mother of Jesus. Mary wraps her mantle a bit closer about her, and we see in her peaceful gaze the depth of her surrender to God.

We feel the light touch of a breeze. How is that possible in this closed room? It grows stronger, and something is pulling our slouched bodies into an upright position. We realize that this is no outer wind, but a spiritual perception, which is growing so strong as to almost block our physical awareness. The wind roars around us and through us, like the breath of God flowing over the waters at creation.

A blazing fire appears, hovering over Mary's head. It

then splits into tongues of flame, one of which descends upon each of us… We feel the fire pass through us, setting mind, heart, and body ablaze…

We rest for a few moments, feeling God's fire burning in our bones, and God's breath breathing in our breath…

The Eucharist

The Eucharist (from the Greek word for 'thanksgiving') is the sacrament most often associated with the work of the priesthood. It is also the sacrament in which we participate most regularly throughout our lives. Most priests celebrate the Eucharist at least once a week, and often more frequently. Also known as Communion or the Lord's Supper, it is the spiritual-physical food which sustains us on our journey, joining us more closely to the Christ, that we may be transmuted through the power of shared existence.

The Eucharist is most often celebrated using unleavened bread and wine, recalling the elements blessed by Jesus of Nazareth at his last supper with his disciples. If possible, the use of these elements helps to preserve the power of that historical link. Some Christian traditions have used leavened bread, grape juice, or water. The Kakure Kirishitan of Japan bless rice, fish, and sake in their communion liturgy. I know a fine priest who, in an emergency, conducted a communion rite with Fritos and orange juice, as that was all that was available.

Likewise, it is a fine thing to have a chalice and paten (cup and plate) which are specially reserved and blessed for use in the Eucharist. However, in case of necessity, anything can be used—even holding a saltine cracker in the palm of one hand, and some drops of water or wine in the other palm. The New Apostolic Church bakes small communion wafers which are already impregnated with three drops of wine, so that the elements are combined and no separate chalice is needed. While this practice does blur the distinction between earthy substance and sustaining fluid, it could prove very useful for travel and other limited situations.

Communion bread can be purchased in most religious supply stores, and will keep for a long time. You can also use matzo or crackers from the supermarket, or any other form of bread. If you are interested in baking your own bread for communion—which can be a lovely extension of the sacrament—recipes are easily available on the internet, and in books (e.g. Tony Begonja, *Eucharistic Bread Baking as Ministry*).

It is also quite possible to celebrate the Eucharist as part of a regular meal, whether on one's own kitchen table, or in a restaurant. A simple consecration and sharing of bread and wine can be part of the supper, just as it was with Jesus and his apostles. When an inquirer asked a Shaker elder why the Shakers do not celebrate the Eucharist, the elder replied, "Oh but we do! We eat together three times a day!"

In the event that physical elements are not available, or circumstances do not allow for outer ceremonial, it is possible to work through the sacrament inwardly, offering our own body and blood as the elements for transmutation in the presence of Christ, which will then be offered to the world through our lives. This is a practice which can be done anywhere, at anytime. My thanks go to bishop Mary Ray of Lawrence, Kansas, who taught me this practice.

Formal liturgies for the Eucharist are easily obtainable, in bookstores and on line. A new priest would do well to study the rites of the Roman, Episcopal, Orthodox, Liberal Catholic, and other churches. Perhaps you will find a rite which resonates with you, or one that you can alter for your purposes. You may want to attend different liturgies, and observe other priests. Some priests like to memorize a favorite rite, while others find memorization distracting, and prefer to work from a written text. Still others prefer to improvise. Regardless, a capable priest should be familiar enough with the inner shape of communion to be able to serve at any moment.

Communion at its most basic is the blessing and sharing of bread and wine. The following gives a simple form of the Eucharist, which can be elaborated as needed. Candles, incense, and a prepared altar are wonderful, but not necessary.

1. The priest empties him/herself, and consciously enters into the presence of Christ. If you are not in a state of realization of the presence of Christ, it will be very difficult to mediate that presence to others. The priest may make this preparation silently, or in spoken prayer, and may also lead others in making similar preparation.

2. If a Bible or other similar text (e.g. the Gospel of Thomas, the Gospel of Philip) is available, the priest or others may read one or more selections from scripture. There are widely available lectionaries, which give a plan of readings throughout the year. These can be helpful in providing access to a wide range of readings, but one should feel free to improvise as needed. One can even open the Bible at random, choosing a passage through bibliomancy, if so moved. The reading may be followed with meditative silence or a short reflection by the priest, if s/he is so inspired. This is not an educational lecture, but an attempt to reach more deeply into the Word.

3. Silent or spoken prayers gather up the intentions of those who have gathered to celebrate communion. This may include traditional prayers like the Lord's Prayer or Hail Mary. This transitional point may also include the recitation of the central story of the Christian Mystery in some form, such as a creed.

4. The bread and wine are blessed and prepared. The priest gives thanks to God, recalling the Mystery of Christ in which we now participate. The priest opens him or herself that s/he may become the very presence of Christ for the blessing, offering, and distribution of these elements. Speaking in the power of Christ, s/he calls down the Holy Spirit to transform the bread and wine into the body and blood, the substance and life of Christ. S/he speaks the words of Jesus, as Jesus: This is my body. This is my blood. S/he prays that this communion may be effective for all those present, and the living and dead who are remembered in prayer.

5. The priest now distributes the bread and wine to each person who wishes to receive. No one who seeks to meet Christ in the sacrament should ever be turned away. Words of blessing, absolution, and/or guidance may be spoken to the communicants in accord with individual inspiration.

6. The priest gathers up the remaining bread and wine. S/he may consume some of it, in proxy communion for those who are not present, or those who are dead. In silent or spoken prayer, s/he offers all those present in body, spirit, or memory, to Christ, to be received by him, just as we have received him in the communion. S/he consciously lifts the totality of our lives to Christ, that he may transform us according to

the Divine Will. When this inner exchange is complete, s/he offers silent or spoken thanksgiving.

7. The priest gives a final blessing, through which
the power of the communion streams out beyond those
present, to the neighborhood, the land, the Earth itself.

If there is bread and/or wine remaining, it should be
reverently reserved until such time as it will be consumed. The consecration of the elements does not go
away after the rite. The reserved elements can be held
on an altar as a focus for prayer and meditation, or carried with one in a small container (to commune oneself
or others, or for spiritual focus, presence, and protection). If consecrated bread and wine spoils and must be
disposed of, it should be burned or buried with
prayers.

The cup and plate used for communion should also
be carefully cleaned. This is more of an inner process
rather than using any special method of cleaning. As
the water rinses down through the sink and drain, you
can imagine the blessing of the Eucharist going with it,
into the water system, and ultimately to the rivers, the
seas, the earth.

Communion increases our union with Christ, and is
a blessing to the earth. It is a gift to be able to celebrate
it as often as possible. If one is physically alone, one is
still joined to the saints, the angels, and all the living
and dead who gather around this mystery. Some priests
have a vocation of primarily hidden intercession
through (physically) solitary communion. Others have
a more public Eucharistic ministry. All that matters is
that one does it.

MEDITATIONS

I invite you to lay aside all cares, and sink deep into meditation for a few moments, resting in God's presence…

In the flickering lamplight, we look around the table at Jesus and our fellow disciples. We have eaten the Passover meal together, and feel the satisfaction of the food and wine which has nourished us, as we recalled the story of our ancestors. A quiet space of calm reflection has come upon us all.

Jesus looks at each of us, and picks up a piece of bread and a cup of wine. He offers a prayer of heartfelt thanks to God. Then he hands us the bread, saying "This is my body…" and the cup saying, "This is my blood…" We each take a bite from the bread, and a sip from the cup.

As this simple food enters us, something strange begins to happen. It is as if a great fire had been lit within us, blazing through us, but without consuming us. The fire burns in our bones, races through our blood, lights our faces. We remember Jesus saying, "I am come to cast fire on the earth…" Speech fails us, and we feel ourselves becoming all flame, purified to be One Body and One Blood with our Lord.

As outer awareness begins to return, we hear Jesus say-

ing to us, "I am among you as one who serves." We know this as our own calling, and let God's fire blaze through us, even more brightly, for a few moments....

Absolution

For some, the subject of absolution quickly conjures up terrifying childhood confessional scenes, but when properly understood, is still very important today. Absolution is often given in a general way in the Eucharist, but some people will find benefit in meeting individually with a priest. In sacramental reconciliation, guilt is released on a spiritual level, even though one often still has to work through the consequences in outer life.

Just as with an old-fashioned confession, the priest has no right to ever speak of the matter of the confession, or to even allude to the fact that there was a confession. Confidentiality is an extremely serious spiritual commitment, if one is going to hear the confessions of others.

Also, the confessional is not counseling. The penitent is offering his or her situation into the hands of Christ. The priest is only there as a physical instrument of this process. For this reason, it can be helpful for both priest and penitent to face an icon of Christ, or for the priest to wear some sign of her office, signifying that she is acting as a priest, and not as an individual.

Sacramental reconciliation can take place anywhere. I have heard confessions in places as unlikely as parking lots and Chinese restaurants. Many modern people are troubled by guilt, and benefit from hearing in a very direct way that they are enveloped in God's compassion and forgiveness.

The format is very simple. Priest and penitent place themselves consciously in the Divine presence, in whatever way is appropriate to the circumstances. The penitent then speaks freely. The priest should not indulge in psychological counseling, but may give a word or two of guidance, or inner work or service to perform to help unravel whatever has been wrought. The priest then speaks in these or similar words: "I absolve you of all your sins, in the name of the Father and of the Son and of the Holy Spirit. Amen." If at all possible, the priest should touch the penitent (on the hand, crown of the head, or temple) when speaking the words.

Rudolf Steiner's Christengemeinschaft expanded this sacrament into "Sacramental Consultation." In Sacramental Consultation, one speaks not only of sin and problems, but of the entire shape of one's life, the questions with which one struggles, the promise and potential one is working to realize. Again, the priest is not present to provide spiritually-coated therapy, but to mediate the presence of Christ, who receives the substance of life that is being offered. If words of absolution are not appropriate, the priest can simply give a blessing.

Another expansion of the sacrament is found in Paul Blighton's rite of "Removal of the Veil." In Blighton's view, there is a veil which indicates our separation from conscious unity with Divinity. One might think of the veil of the Temple of Jerusalem, which hid the Holy of Holies, until it ripped open at the time of the crucifixion of Jesus. In Blighton's rite, a trained priest removes the veil in a radical act of absolution, so that the person may begin to enter freely into their own Holy of Holies. Every act of absolution mirrors this, to a lesser degree.

MEDITATIONS

I invite you to lay aside all cares, and sink deep into meditation for a few moments, resting in God's presence....

It is Sunday night, and we are with some other disciples of Jesus, locked in the upper room of one of our friends' houses. Jesus was executed on Friday, and now his body has gone missing. Mary Magdalene told us a story of seeing him alive in the garden, but grief can play tricks on the best of us... And Mary, well, she was very fond of Jesus...

If the authorities killed Jesus, how do we know that we are not next? Especially with crazy tales of coming back from the dead, to aggravate matters. Fear has gotten the best of us, and we have shut ourselves in, until we can come up with a better plan, or get out of town.

A strange light, coming from no-where, begins to shine in the room. Even the dark places and shadows seem to emit an almost burning radiance. Our hearts beat fast, our breath catches, and eyes flicker around the room. Suddenly, we see Jesus, in flesh and blood, not any ethereal vision, standing in our midst. As if to answer our question, he holds up his hands, and hot red blood drips from the wounds onto the floor. We don't know whether to faint from fear, or cry

43

with joy. Jesus looks at us with a smile, and says, "Peace be with you. As the Father sends me, so I now send you."

He opens his arms wide, as our hands reach toward him. He breathes out, and the breath flows through us, until we are only and always Breath. He says, "Receive the Holy Spirit….. If you forgive the sins of any, they are forgiven. If you bind the sins of any, they are bound."

Jesus is gone again, but still breathing in our breath. We breathe for a few moments….

Anointing

Anointing and/or the laying on of hands for healing has long been a part of sacramental practice. The first thing to remember is that we usually do not know what really constitutes healing or balance. In working with another person, our fundamental inner gesture should be an opening to the Spirit, which will then act in whatever way is needed, without our attempt to control or direct it.

As with all the sacraments, the basic form is extremely simple. The priest anoints the person with blessed oil, while saying something along the lines of "I anoint you for healing, in the name of the Father and of the Son and of the Holy Spirit. Amen." The anointing is most often on the forehead or crown, but other body points may be included as appropriate. One can also lay hands on or near the body. Saints and angels often associated with healing (such as the Archangel Raphael) may be invoked. The priest ends with thanksgiving for the Divine presence.

Anointing may be done for any person who feels an illness or imbalance on any level. As this can apply to most of us, most of the time, some priests routinely offer anointing to anyone who wishes to receive, after communion. This sacrament has often been associated with the "last rites" given to a person when death is expected soon. In such a case, one would typically combine the anointing with absolution and communion. If a person is very sick and cannot easily receive communion, it can be given in the form of one drop of consecrated wine or water in the mouth.

In today's alternative spiritual world, there are many esoteric healing techniques, such as Reiki, Therapeutic Touch, Attunement, and so on. If one is familiar with the patterns used in these techniques, they can be easily combined with sacramental anointing. They do not make the anointing better or more powerful, but can give the mind and the hands something to keep them busy while opening to Spirit. As bishop Lloyd Meeker told his Attunement students, you can mess up the techniques and hand placements to your heart's content, and the healing will still work, as long as your intent is correct.

Closely related to anointing is the practice of exorcism, the removal of a foreign spiritual entity which has lodged in a person. Mercifully, such cases are relatively rare. Exorcism is not lightly undertaken, and is best learned (if necessary) by in-person work with an experienced priest.

MEDITATIONS

I invite you to lay aside all cares, and sink deep into meditation for a few moments, resting in God's presence....

We are standing by a dusty road, with many others, waiting for Jesus who is said to be coming. Each of us feels our infirmity in some way, the suffering that seems inherent in living, an ancient twistedness we can never seem to completely unknot. We don't know quite why we believe this teacher can help us, but nonetheless we are here, waiting....

The noise and movement of the crowd signal Jesus' approach. There are so many people—how will Jesus even know we are here? Suddenly the crowd opens, and without even thinking we reach through, touching Jesus' garment.

At the moment we touch him, a tremendous power flows through us, and we feel suffused with peace, forgiveness, and healing on all levels. We know the truth of who we are as God's beloved children, and the truth of who we may become. Jesus turns, looks us right in the eye with deep compassion, and smiles. It is as if the crowd has melted away and we see only Jesus. He says, "Your faith has healed you. Go in peace."

For a few moments, we let that deep peace overflow through us, pouring out unconditionally into the world....

Funerals

Anointing is properly the sacrament of those approaching death, especially when combined with absolution and communion. The funeral or memorial service is not a sacrament, but is a liturgical service which most priests will be called upon to perform from time to time.

Traditional forms for funerals can be found in all liturgical manuals, but you can create a simple service of prayer, scripture readings, and remembrance of the deceased, with a final commendation of the person's soul to Christ (or more simply to the Divine, if they did not practice Christianity). The focus of a Christian memorial should not be on the loss of the person, but on the assurance of resurrection and life in Christ. Simplicity and dignity are important. If at all possible, it is best to wait several days after death, to be certain that the person's attachment to their prior physical body is at least largely loosened.

After death, the person is still a vital part of the community, and should be particularly remembered at celebrations of the Eucharist, at which the dead are always present, even if not perceived. I have also found Rudolf Steiner's suggestion of reading to the dead to be most helpful. Steiner suggested that one call the dead person into consciousness and then read to them aloud from spiritual texts, most especially the Gospel of John. This practice can be done alone, or in a group, with each person taking a small passage in turn.

If a person is having significant difficulty in crossing through death, there are ways of assisting them—but this is not a manual on dealing with the dead. In her book, *Through the Gates of Death*, Dion Fortune provides a small Christian liturgy which I have found very effective in assisting those who have died in sudden or traumatic ways.

MEDITATIONS

I invite you to lay aside all cares, and sink deep into meditation for a few moments, resting in God's presence…

We sit on the rocky isle of Patmos, listening to the waves and watching our elderly teacher, the apostle John, who has been exiled to this remote place, because of his witness to Jesus. He sits at the entrance to the cave where he sleeps, deep in prayer. His eyelids flutter, and his long white beard blows gently in the wind. It is Sunday, and we have all just shared in the body and blood of our Lord.

We are struck by the sense of a powerful sound, which seems to be above our normal range of hearing. It rings through our heads, and we turn with John to see what is happening. As soon as we turn, we fall flat upon the ground at the vision, some of us fainting dead away.

Jesus stands before us, shining brighter than the sun. We remember John telling us how he once shone like this upon Mount Tabor. He is in a long white robe, bound with gold, and he stands in the middle of seven golden candlesticks which also blaze with light. His eyes are like fire, and his hair brilliant white. Even his feet shine—and his voice is more powerful than the sea in storm. In his right hand are seven stars, and in vision, we see a sharp sword coming from his mouth.

Fear seizes every aspect of our being. Even our normally fearless teacher trembles. But Jesus reaches out, and gently touches John. He speaks, "Fear not, I am the first and the last, and the living one. I died and behold I am alive forevermore. I hold the keys of death and Hades."

We feel our fear evaporate, as the light of the Lord, brilliant beyond all color, streams through us. We let his light and life move through us for a few moments, giving thanks to him as his love releases all that binds us…

Matrimony

People in our culture traditionally call a priest for baptism, marriage, and burial—threshold points in our lives. Marriage is an interesting sacrament, as it was the last of the usual sacraments to be regarded as such. Also, according to traditional sacramental theology, the ministers of the sacrament are the couple, who offer it to one another. The role of the priest is not strictly necessary, and is only to witness and bless the union. The form of the sacrament is simply each partner's declaration of intent to the other, with all the rest (rings, candles, long ceremonies, etc) as decorative additions.

An important distinction is that between the sacrament of matrimony, and the legal contract of state-sanctioned marriage. In the United States, the two often, but not always, coincide. It is my view that it is best for a priest to restrict herself to blessing the sacramental marriage. If the couple wishes to be married in the eyes of the state, they can have a separate ceremony conducted by the appropriate government official. A priest of Christ is not an agent of the government, and should not be stating "By the power vested in me by the State of X...." This is a confusion of roles. If a priest takes the position of only blessing sacramental marriages, without getting involved in the legal side of things, she needs to be sure that the couple clearly understands this is the case. On the other hand, if a priest chooses to sign the legal marriage license, she needs to be certain that she meets all the local requirements to do so, as these vary widely.

A priest who serves alternative communities may well be called upon to conduct sacramental marriages for those who are not currently able to marry under the law, such as same-sex couples, or poly-marriages of more than two people. As long as there is no pretense to conducting a legally binding marriage, and it is clear that this is only a religious/sacramental blessing of an arrangement among consenting adults, there is no problem in doing so. Discussion with the partners about their understanding of the spiritual structure of their marriage will lead the priest to appropriate readings and ritual language. (For example, one might use the story of David and Jonathan for a marriage of two men, or alchemical symbolism of salt, sulphur, and mercury for a triad.)

Closely related to marriage, a priest may often be called upon to bless other states of life. A person may be newly single due to divorce or death of a spouse, or may be taking on a commitment to celibacy, or a new form of work, or a spiritual vow (for example, a peace activist who wants to make a vow of nonviolence). No one form of life is privileged—not marriage, celibacy, or any other way—and all ethical ways of living can receive sacramental blessing. For that reason, instead of a meditation on marriage in particular, I offer the following on the beatitudes, which can shape any form of life.

MEDITATIONS

I invite you to lay aside all cares, and sink deep into meditation for a few moments, resting in God's presence....

It is a beautiful warm day, with a clear blue sky stretched above us. We are walking quickly, in a gathering crowd of people, toward the outskirts of town. Word has it that the teacher Jesus and his disciples are here. We have heard of this odd rabbi from Galilee, and his ragtag band of followers, and the healings they have worked in other villages. We want to see for ourselves.

As we come into the countryside, there is a tall hill before us, where lots of other people have already gathered. As we look up toward the top of the hill, there is a man in the center, in a simple robe, who is surely Jesus. He looks toward us, and we feel a deep recognition, as if we had always known him. We quickly find a place on the hillside, within earshot of Jesus.

Jesus sits down, and begins to teach. It is as if each of his words is a stream of light, reaching into us, illumining and changing us:

"Blessed are the poor in spirit, for theirs is the kingdom of heaven...

Blessed are those who mourn,
for they shall be comforted...
Blessed are the meek, for they shall inherit the earth...
Blessed are those who hunger and thirst for righteousness,
for they shall be satisfied...
Blessed are the merciful, for they shall obtain mercy...
Blessed are the pure in heart, for they shall see God...
Blessed are the peacemakers,
for they shall be called children of God...
Blessed are those who are persecuted
for righteousness' sake,
for theirs is the kingdom of heaven..."
We rest for a few moments, as we allow these blessings to
work within us...

Proclaiming the Word

In the early 20th century, the Polish National Catholic Church added to the sacramental tradition by declaring the proclamation of the gospel, in the liturgy, as a sacrament. There is much to ponder in the power of sacred words, spoken forth with intention. After all, Christ is said to be the Word of God. This use of the Word is not an attempt to educate, inform, or dogmatize, but simply to connect to the stream of power flowing through the spoken scripture. I have experienced this strongly when standing in the choir of a monastery chanting psalms—I couldn't have told you much about the content, but these ancient words carried me deep into an experience of the Divine. At other times, content does matter, and one experiences the recited Word as speaking directly to the soul.

We experience our lives as narrative, and find meaning through stories. In the gospel, we are given a larger story—that of the life, death, and resurrection of the Christ—in which to inscribe ourselves.

In traditional deacon ordinations, the new deacon is told that s/he is to "read the gospel for the living and for the dead." Just as other sacraments touch the invisible worlds of the dead, the saints, the angels and other spirits, so does the proclamation of the word. When our voice carries the sacred text out into the world with living power, the effect can reach far beyond what we can immediately perceive.

Beyond the use of specific sacred texts in a liturgical context, we might ponder how the Divine Word works through our speech and language, throughout our daily life. How can our words become sacramental expression at all times (or at least more often)?

MEDITATIONS

I invite you to lay aside all cares, and sink deep into meditation for a few moments, resting in God's presence...

It is the morning of the Sabbath, and we are sitting on rough benches in a small stone synagogue in Nazareth. The men wrap their prayer-shawls a bit tighter, and sway with the prayer. We feel the pathos, as our true allegiance is acknowledged, even under the iron fist of Roman rule.

Jesus is home today, and sits among us. We have known his family all his life. His father, Joseph, would be proud to see how he has grown. We have heard reports that he has become some kind of wandering healer, but people do talk... At least he comes home to see his mother...

Jesus is invited up to read. He takes the scroll, and moves the pointer carefully until he finds the place he is looking for. We wonder what he is doing—this is surely not the appointed reading... His voice rings out like a clear bell:

"The Spirit of the Lord is upon me, because he has anointed me to preach good news to the poor. He has sent me to proclaim release to the captives and recovering of sight to the blind, to set at liberty those who are oppressed, to proclaim the acceptable year of the Lord."

The familiar words of Isaiah carry an unusual power today, as if they were being spoken for the first time. An odd vibration fills both the air, and our bodies. Everyone is looking at Jesus, who looks slowly around the room, making eye contact with each person. The faintest hint of a smile plays at the corner of his lips.

Jesus speaks again, "Today this scripture has been fulfilled in your hearing." A feeling of awe falls down upon us, as we gaze on this simple man... We rest in this awe for a few moments...

The Mandatum

The Mandatum is the traditional name for the sacramental practice of the washing of feet. It is the Latin word for 'commandment', and refers to Jesus' instruction to the disciples, after washing their feet, that they should do as he has done. In many Catholic, Orthodox, and Anglican churches, this practice is only observed once a year on Holy Thursday (often called Maundy Thursday for just this reason), immediately prior to Easter. However, some Protestant churches observe the mandatum more frequently, and I once visited an independent sacramental parish in Chicago which did it every week, as a regular part of the liturgy.

The practice is extremely simple, and consists only in washing feet. Ideally, each person present should have the opportunity to both wash and be washed. It is a humbling and often emotionally moving experience, embodying a commitment to love and serve one another. One can elaborate the ceremony in various ways, such as anointing feet after washing them. Prayers and readings can be found in printed liturgies for Holy Thursday.

Even if the mandatum is observed rarely or not at all, in terms of ceremonial practice, one would do well to ponder how its inner gesture can be lived in our relationships with those around us.

MEDITATIONS

I invite you to lay aside all cares, and sink deep into meditation for a few moments, resting in God's presence....

It is Passover and we are gathered with Jesus in the Upper Room. The clouds have been gathering around our little community, and we are troubled when we think of what the future may bring. One of our number, Judas, had strange words with Jesus during the meal, then left. But we are comforted to be together for this sacred feast. Remembering how our ancestors were delivered, hope stirs faintly within us.

Following dinner, Jesus rises and lays aside his outer garment. He wraps himself in a towel, pours water in a bowl, and tells us he is going to wash our feet. This is a menial task performed only by slaves, or hired servants. How can our teacher wash our feet?

Peter can always be counted upon to speak our thoughts, and he asks Jesus how he can do this. Jesus replies, "What I am doing you do not know now, but afterward you will understand." Peter grows more insistent, "You will never wash my feet!" Jesus looks at Peter (and all of us) with infinite patience, and replies, "If I do not wash you, you have no part in me."

Peter recovers himself and allows Jesus to lift his feet over the basin, saying, "Lord, not my feet only but my hands and my head!" Jesus says, "If you have already bathed, you have no need to wash, except for your feet…" Jesus now comes to each of us, one by one. We feel his gentle care, and the embarrassing intimacy of the moment, as he washes our feet in the cool water, and dries them carefully….

Having put away the basin and towel, and slipping his robe back on, Jesus turns to us, and we feel a serious intensity from him, as if there is not much time for us to grasp all he is trying to convey. He speaks: "Do you know what I have done to you? You call me teacher and Lord, and you are right, for so I am. If I then, your Lord and teacher, have washed your feet, you also ought to wash one another's feet. For I have given you an example, that you also should do as I have done to you."

We rest for a few moments, feeling the last of the water drying on our feet, as we ponder what our teacher has done…

Holy Orders

Holy Orders is the sacrament through which the line of priesthood in this tradition is passed on to others. Whether it originated with Jesus and the apostles is historically interesting, but inwardly beside the point. There is a line of priesthood which connects to the reality of the Christ, and it works.

Just as one inherits genetic strengths and weaknesses from one's physical parents, so strengths and weaknesses are passed along in such a priesthood transmission. One benefits from all the positive work of many spiritual ancestors over the centuries, but also must engage with the distortions and problems passed through the tradition.

Ordination has often been tied to obedience to hierarchy, specific jurisdictions, and membership and service in a particular church. This is no longer necessary. The priesthood simply is. One need not belong to anything, or give it any label. One's service is the mediation of the power, love, and wisdom of the Christ (the divine Child of Light) through one's daily circumstances. This may look outwardly priestly in some cases, and not at all so, in others. Many 'stealth priests' may fly completely under the radar.

Traditionally, the actual sacrament of orders was often preceded by a number of 'minor orders' which participated in the grace of priesthood to a lesser degree. The names, number, and order of these minor ordinations vary, but the most common list is: Cleric, Doorkeeper, Reader, Exorcist (or Healer), Acolyte, and Subdeacon. This process can be quite helpful in training a new priest, and marking stages along the way, as each minor order reflects a facet of the work of priest-hood. For example, the order of Reader is the natural time to learn about sacred scripture, and the power of the Word; the order of Exorcist gives an opportunity to engage healing, exorcism, and basic pastoral psychology; the order of Acolyte provides time for liturgical/ritual training; and so on.

Unless one has academic inclinations, or the desire to join what Roger Williams deprecatingly called "the hireling ministry," there is no need to haul oneself off to years of seminary. One can learn to be a fine priest through simple apprenticeship to another, sustained spiritual discipline, and hard practice.

The sacrament of ordination is usually divided into deacon, priest, and bishop. Sometimes, there are added intermediate steps such as archdeacon or archpriest. However, as it is one sacrament, and not three (or five or seven, or however many steps), some have taught that the sacrament is actually received in fullness at deacon, and then opened out in wider service at priest and bishop. These orders fit together like Russian dolls, with each one containing all those below it. Thus, if one is simply ordained directly to the priesthood, one does not miss out on the diaconate or minor orders, as they are contained therein. The same goes for consecration directly to the order of bishop.

It is the role of a bishop to teach and ordain others, to pass this line of priesthood along into the future. Each bishop has to discern what training and preparation are needed in any given case, and whether to proceed step by step, or move someone forward more quickly. It is a matter of listening for inner guidance, and responding. It is my opinion that bishops should not bind their candidates to themselves through promises of obedience or any other means. A candidate is free to continue working with the bishop, or to go away at any stage.

The priesthood of Christ is not a job. It is a way of life. Very few independent sacramental priests will ever have a community willing to pay them for their availability. Rather, most will have mundane jobs to support themselves. This situation is actually a tremendous grace, as it pours the priesthood (in silent and sneaky ways) into all sorts of different professions and ways of life.

Our duty as priests is to listen for the Divine, and respond. That is all.

Ordinations tend to be complex and often beautiful affairs, with long litanies, invocations, questions, addresses, and much general carrying on. It is traditional to convey all ordinations within the context of the Eucharist, if at all possible. Nonetheless, all that is required is that the bishop lays hands on the head of the candidate, invoking the Holy Spirit to fill the candidate, that they might receive the grace of the order being conferred (whether cleric, bishop, or anything in between). "Receive the Holy Spirit, for the office and work of a priest (or whatever order)." The ordination is always done by the Holy Spirit. The bishop simply provides the physical point of connection. Only one hand is often used for minor orders and the diaconate, with two hands for priest and bishop. The head (and sometimes the hands) of the candidate are frequently anointed.

The inner process activated by an ordination usually continues for days or even weeks. One simply has to be attentive and to go with the process as much as possible. Resistance is futile! The grace of the ordination will continue to unfold and change over the course of one's life, often in surprising ways. Being a priest in the lineage of the Christ can be a very odd journey, but never boring!

MEDITATIONS

As we prepare to meet the Christ in this blessing today, I invite you to lay aside all cares, and sink deep into meditation for a few moments, resting in God's presence...

It is night, and we are climbing up the slope of a small mountain in Galilee. Some of us have lanterns, but it is hard to keep from bumping into stones and scrubby bushes. Jesus our teacher, who was brutally executed, has been appearing to us. He is no ghost, for he eats and bleeds and touches us. But we are far from understanding what is happening. Nonetheless, he has instructed some of our number to summon us to this mountain. Thus, doubters and faithful alike, we climb the hill.

As we come around a large stone which had blocked our view, we see the entrance to a small cave, and Jesus standing quietly in the dark waiting for us. Our lanterns shine on him and catch the outlines of his features and the dark blood of his wounds. Jesus speaks to us: "All authority in heaven and in earth has been given to me. Go therefore and make disciples of all nations, baptizing them in the name of the Father, and of the Son, and of the Holy Spirit, teaching them to observe all that I have commanded you; and lo, I am with you always, to the close of the age."

With these words, we feel a deep pounding within the earth, and the vibration begins to enter our bodies and move upward through them, in a feeling of exaltation we have never known. A cloud of shining bright light forms above Jesus, and begins to descend down upon us all, engulfing the whole cave and surrounding area. For a few moments, we are lost in the clear white light...

The cloud lifts up, and disappears, leaving us disoriented, sitting dazed on the cave floor. Jesus is no longer with us, but we hear his words within us, "Lo, I am with you always..."

CHAPTER THREE:

The Spiritual Life

The inner connections to the reality of Christ, forged by an ordination into this tradition, are permanent, and cannot be eradicated, no matter how much they are ignored. Nonetheless, you will be a much more effective priest if you nurture the grace you have been given through the practice of a spiritual discipline. First and foremost is the regular practice of the sacraments themselves, especially the Eucharist. Through exercising your priesthood on a frequent basis, you will become ever more deeply inscribed into the priesthood of Christ, due to his working through you in the rites.

The Breviary

There is a long tradition of priests and other vowed spiritual workers in the Christian tradition being obligated to the breviary, a formal set of daily prayers, assigned to particular hours of the day, especially morning and evening. While as a free priest you carry no such obligation, you might find it good advice. There are many breviaries, traditional and experimental, available through the publishing houses of the mainstream churches. You can even find a few published esoteric breviaries, such as that created by Rudolf Steiner for the priests of the Christengemeinschaft.

However, it is not necessary to follow a published breviary, as it is quite simple to create your own. The heart of the practice is usually the recitation of the psalms, the ancient poetry of Jewish scripture. Many people have reactions against the psalms, upon first encounter. These odd poems carry a lot of emotion, and sometimes disturbing thoughts and images. Virtually any inner state which a human being could experience is contained therein. Over time, you begin to experience the psalms as a journey into our own mixed and fractured experience as we struggle with the Divine. No one is asking you to believe that the images of God are accurate—rather, the psalms are an invitation to open compassionately to share in the human experience described therein, held out in all its raw honesty before God.

To create your own breviary practice, you will want to pick a time (morning, or evening, or both, are traditional choices) when you can spend ten to twenty minutes in prayer every day. Begin by quieting yourself. You might light a candle, or set out an icon. Then, recite or chant two or three psalms, or portions of psalms, if they are particularly lengthy. If you choose to chant, it does not have to be elaborate unless you are so inclined. A simple monotone will do. (For help with chanting, see *Singing the Psalms* by Cynthia Bourgeault.) Follow the psalmody with silence, and then a short reading from scripture, and/or a text from the tradition (such as a saint's life, mystical theology, etc.). The reading is not for information, but as a stimulus to meditative pondering. After such pondering, you can close with a prayer, such as the *Lord's Prayer*, or *Hail Mary*.

Most published breviaries arrange the psalms and readings to accord with the time of the day, the day of the week, and the season of the church year. This can be helpful, if one is working with those rhythms, but such complexity is not needed. You can simply begin with Psalms 1, 2, and 3, and then keep going sequentially until you finish them, and cycle back to Psalm 1 again. The readings can be handled in a similar way—going slowly through a particular gospel, or text, until you finish it. Whichever method you use, you will probably notice that highly appropriate themes have a funny way of coming to the surface at just the right time.

A priest may choose to engage in other forms of prayer throughout the day—centering prayer, various meditative disciplines, times of intercession, the rosary, the *Jesus prayer*, and so on. You can experiment with types of prayer, and find those which work for you. Fine suggestions can be found in The *Wisdom Way of Knowing* by Cynthia Bourgeault, and *Tools Matter for Practicing the Spiritual Life* by Mary Margaret Funk. A practice does not have to be complicated or arcane to be highly effective. I once asked a very radiant and holy man about his spiritual practice. He replied that he simply invited Christ to sit with him every morning on his bus ride to work. "Sometimes we talk, mostly we just sit together, but that's our time, every day."

Whatever form it takes, a regular practice gives at least a few minutes per day when other concerns are pushed aside, and we become available to God. The grace which comes through keeping our inner connection strong then can work itself out through the circumstances of our daily life. We can also be helped in our formation as free priests through a consideration of the Rosicrucian Rules, and the vows historically taken by religious orders.

The Rosicrucian Rules

In the course of pondering on the spiritual life of the independent priest, I have been drawn back repeatedly to the rules of the Rosicrucian fraternity found in the *Fama Fraternitas* (first published in 1614, although probably written a few years earlier—the whole text can be found online). The *Fama Fraternitas* and related 17th century texts purport to represent the history and teachings of a secretive Christian mystical order known as the Fraternity of the Rose Cross, founded by Christian Rosenkreutz. Most scholars view this 'history' as a legend given shape by a 17th century Lutheran pastor, Johann Valentin Andreae. Whatever the truth of Rosicrucian origins, the story and its associated symbols have deeply impacted Western esotericism ever since. To give credit where credit is due, I heard Christopher Bamford refer to the potential of the Rosicrucian rules as a modern spiritual guide, some years ago. Although he was working in a different context, he sparked my imagination. The rules are as follows:

One: that none of them should profess any other thing, than to cure the sick, and that for free. This first rule truly says it all. Our primary focus is an unreserved dedication to service, the curing of the sick (who may well include ourselves)—no matter at what level the sickness or imbalance may be found. If this is not done, all else is for naught, and will ultimately circle back to an unhealthy self-centeredness. As the core commitment of the inner priesthood, it also gives a reason why the priesthood is found in many guises. As my teacher and friend Mark Nicholas Whitehead likes to say, the mantle of priesthood (those truly able to mediate grace and move the power of the Spirit) has largely left mainstream religions, and moved to odd people like us. In time, our ways may become so rigid that it moves again—the job has to get done and the Spirit will use whoever is available, however unlikely they may seem. Some may carry a visible priesthood, while others will mediate the Light of the Christ through their "secular" work, family life, play, and other more hidden (and sometimes more effective) activities.

Moreover, the cure of the sick is for free. Grace is a gift freely given. The spiritual life is not a commodity to be bought and sold. Remember what Jesus did to the moneychangers in the temple? This does not mean that there is anything wrong with money, or that people should not be compensated for their time. Most of us have the luxury of supporting ourselves in work that is not outwardly identified as priestly, so that we are free to engage in spiritual work without requesting monetary compensation. This gives us great freedom, as our conscience cannot be put over a barrel by those (congregation, bishop, church) who pay our salary and guarantee our pension. Monetary offerings should carry the quality of gift, not requirement. If money stands in the way of service, it must stand aside. What we have to offer must be openly available to all, regardless of possessions or wealth.

Two: None of the posterity should be constrained to wear one certain kind of habit, but therein to follow the custom of the country. There is no need for us to run around in robes and clerical collars, or to lead a certain kind of life. (Nonetheless, I am a true believer in bishop John Michael Greer's dictrum that any religion worth belonging to should come with funny hats.) We can be a spiritual leaven within any culture, any profession, in any way of life. We can be the stay-at-home mom whose stove becomes an alchemical altar of transmutation, whether her family realizes it or not. We can be the nurse who delivers healing grace with every pill or injection. We can be the factory worker whose simple presence changes the quality of life for those around him. Then again, we may be a visible priest in a goofy outfit, handing out communion, doing weddings, etc. We don't know how we will be used—we simply offer ourselves for what is needful. The time is past for the traditional arrangement of one or two clergy, and a whole congregation of laity. We are learning to delve deeper into the mystery of priesthood, and to find how all people may live this mystery, in an infinite variety of ways. Maybe ordination should be the natural trajectory for the baptized person.

Three: That every year upon the Day C, they should meet together at the House of the Holy Spirit, or to write the cause of his absence. In a free priesthood, there is no longer any need for a structure or formal organization. Spiritual transmission, person to person, is   enough. Cooperation and support is still critically important, but can happen in free-form, ad hoc, anarchic ways, as the need   arises. The Rosicrucian sisters and brothers must meet together, or give an excuse— but this happens in the House of the Holy Spirit, not in a temple made by hands. (The meaning of "the Day C" is   much debated, but often held to refer to the day of Pentecost, reinforcing that the meeting is in the power of the Spirit,   regardless of earthly separations.) We learn to trust and to live from those inner connections which enliven us, rather than outward recognition and approval, fancy titles, organizational   identity, proper educational degrees, tax-exempt status, and so on.

Four: Every brother should look out for a worthy person, who after his decease should succeed him. Transmission is critically important. As bishop Lloyd Meeker liked to say, blessings are not given to us for us, but through us to others, and through others to us. What we receive, we must pass on, after having fed and increased it out of our own being. An old magical tradition, found in many places, indicates that an initiate must transmit to at least one other person. In another 17th   century Rosicrucian document, *The Chymical Wedding*, Christian Rosenkreutz must release the doorkeeper, and serve in his place   until someone comes along and releases him in turn. Passing along the grace, power, and reality of what we have been given to even one person can be a tall order, but some wind up with responsibility for many more than one. One hopes to see each successor find more profound realization and service than his/her teacher. Otherwise, how can an inner transmission grow?

Five: The word CR should be their seal, mark, and character. CR or Christian Rosenkreutz is not only the seal and mark of the sisters and brothers, but their very character. Has our spiritual identity penetrated us that deeply, moving and changing us at the level of habits and unconscious responses? Christian Rosenkreutz is the legendary founder of the order, but also an image of any spiritual pilgrim or initiate in the Christian inner tradition. His first name marks him as belonging to Christ, and his surname refers to the symbol of the Rose Cross—spirit blooming upon the four-fold cross of the material, elemental world, the unity of God and physical existence. Also, for some spiritual workers, CR has proven to be a profound inner teacher, even if he never lived in outer history.

Six: The fraternity should remain secret one hundred years. The final rule reminds us that much of our most important work happens in silence and in ways that are hidden even from us. One hundred years later the fruits may be seen, although we will have long since passed on. We take the long view, without attachment to any recognition in the short term (recognition that might prove dangerous to us, anyhow).

Taking Vows

Initiation is one of those words with so many meanings as to be almost inevitably misleading. Depending on your background and current practice, initiation may mean many things to you, all of which are surely valid within their context.

One view of initiation which applies well to the independent priest comes from the noted early 20th century occultist Violet Mary Firth, better known as Dion Fortune. In addition to running an occult school (the Society of the Inner Light), Dion Fortune also founded an esoteric church (the Guild of the Master Jesus, later re-named the Church of the Graal), and was said to carry a spiritual lineage after the order of Melchizedek. To Dion Fortune, initiation was primarily concerned with our offering of our spiritual dedication to the Inner Planes or the Masters (or the Saints or to the Divine). The inner powers then proceed to test our dedication, and eventually (hopefully) will accept it. All ritual forms and elaborate ceremonial are only there to aid and support this process. One can easily see the parallels to ordination.

In an unpublished paper written for students who were preparing for ceremonial initiation, Dion Fortune wrote:

"It is the shifting of the central point of our universe which constitutes dedication. We cease to be self-centered and become God-centered. This leads to a complete change in our attitude towards Life. We no longer spend all our time wondering what Life has to give us; we begin to ask ourselves whether we are lifting our share of the world's burden, whether we are adequately filling our place in the cosmic organism. We have ceased to be solitary individuals, struggling to maintain ourselves in a hostile world, our hand against every man and every man's hand against us; we have become brothers to the stars and sisters to the elements. All things are working with us to the common end— the manifestation of Life in its fullness. No longer are we struggling, solitary; we are sweeping onwards in a great tide of Life, gathering momentum as we go.

> *Our change of attitude has led to our being caught up in*
> *the great tide setting God-ward, a tide*
> *'Too full for sound or foam,*
> *When that which draws from out the boundless deep*
> *Turns again home.'"*

The intensity of such dedication is perhaps easier to handle if refracted through different lenses, so that we can ponder on how it takes form in different aspects of our being. In my own inner work, I have found it most useful to approach dedication through a series of spiritual vows. The concept of a vow is useful, I think, as the core commitments of groups ranging from Christian religious orders to pagan initiatic fraternities have been encapsulated in vows. We will break down dedication into eleven vows, which give us something a bit more concrete to work with, rather than abstract dedication. I doubt any of us will ever live up completely to such ideals, but that is all the more reason to pledge ourselves to strive toward them. Also, we come to transformation in the vows not by beating ourselves into some kind of moral submission, but by increasingly opening to the grace of the Spirit acting in us, making us more than we ever suspected we could be.

Obedience to the Mystery

The first vow of a neophyte is obedience to the Divine Spirit, or to the call of the Mystery. Obedience is a word that many of us rightly revolt against, based on our experience with our families and religious backgrounds. But the obedience which stands at the opening of the path is not enforced from without, but is freely offered from within. If we are not willing to lay aside the preferences and ambitions of our personality, in order to listen deeply for how the Mystery of All Things longs to be expressed in our life, we will not go far upon the path. Obedience to the Divine is also the vow we will assign to the end of the path, for here (as is so often the case) the end lies hidden within the beginning. If we truly become responsive to the Spirit, to God, in every moment, all the rest will follow naturally.

The fact that that the neophyte vow is also the final vow should remind us of the seriousness of embarking upon the journey, at all. In a first degree initiation rite from the tradition of Dion Fortune, the candidate is admonished that if she takes one step upon the path, she has committed to coming to the end of the path eventually, whether in this life or a future one—and has volunteered for Life to push her or him continually in that direction.

Service

Having made our neophyte vow to strive to be true to the deepest and best that we find in the core of our being, we pass on to a consideration of our life on the Earth, the physical world in both its inner and outer aspects. Any would-be priest must come to terms with the physical world and life therein. "This can hardly be stressed enough for it is the refusal to come down to Earth, literally, that is the cause of the bulk of spiritual pathology—the root of sin, disease, ignorance. It is the real blasphemy, a rejection of the work of the Father in Heaven, a rejection of the Universe...." (Gareth Knight, *Practical Guide to Qabalistic Symbolism*, vol. II, page10)

The physical world and its challenges are the thrust-block, the resistance that wakes us up to the spiritual path. The vow of service can be assigned here—reaching the point where we have not only control of our outer lives for our own purposes, but dedicate our outer lives and inner work to helping others and the world; as with obedience, this is not service which we are forced to render, but service given freely, infused with love and joy.

Purity

We then move to the watery plane of emotional life, where we are plunged into deep baptismal renewal. One might think of traditional depictions of the Jordan river as inhabited by dragons (like our emotions) and when Christ was baptized, it blazed with fire (purification, infusion of spiritual power and harmony). Note the conjunction of fire and water—like water and oil in most baptismal ceremonies. Our emotions become accurate organs of perception, and naturally (without force) turned more and more toward the Good. The vow here is purity of heart, the right ordering of our emotional and relational life—without the manipulative twistedness so often present. When our emotions are truly able to offer us accurate information about others and the world, rather than just reflecting back to us our own issues, in the guise of others, we can relate to others in a whole new way.

Harmlessness

Following on, we come to the realm of the mind. The danger here is that we will become attached to our particular ideas and conceptions, whether spiritual or otherwise, and will attempt to enforce them upon others. This can take the form of everything from religious fundamentalism to the administrative evil of corporate management. However, truth needs no violence to defend it, and is only distorted by such. Thus, we vow nonviolence or harmlessness in our service, so that our spiritual warriorship brings only healing. Of course, as with a surgeon, there may have to be wounding in order to heal, but this must be done with extraordinarily careful, conscious, directed effort. How this extends into difficult issues like self-defense and war is for each person to wrestle with.

Universal Citizenship

Next we can consider our emotional life on a higher arc, the pressure nudging us to develop, grow, to evolve. Part of this evolutionary pressure is the release of our limited identifications with our families, ethnic backgrounds, nations of origin, etc. All people are the chosen people of God. We let go of our narrow, crystallized identities and embrace an ever-more universal citizenship, the realization that everyone from our friends to our enemies, stars to shrubs to spiders, are our relations. Thus, we vow a commitment to such cosmic sister/brotherhood.

Poverty

Having worked through these realms, we are carried into the place of sacrifice, where dedication comes to an often very pointed focus, where one gives up the lesser, to unconditionally serve the greater. This is the place of the Unreserved Dedication, vowing oneself for a lifetime, or more than a lifetime, holding nothing back. "Father, into thy hands I commend my spirit." Here we make the vow of poverty, dedicating all that one has and will receive into the service of the Divine. The esoteric priestess Sara Greer (who writes as Clare Vaughn) pointed out to me that if "poverty" is a difficult concept for some, this could be seen as boundless generosity. One's life goes through a reversal—the *Hanged Man* of the Tarot is a picture of the initiate priest—no longer living from the outer personality but from the spark of the Divine Spirit within. We should note that, traditionally, the priest has the right to sacrifice his or her self, interests, and possessions—but not the right to sacrifice anyone else. So, if your high-minded spiritual idealism is leading you to sacrifice your spouse or children, you should seriously pause and consider whether you are truly following the direction of Spirit.

Conversion of Life

Following on our freely offered sacrifice, all that is inappropriate or no longer needed begins to break down, in order that the energy locked into these patterns can be released into more useful forms. We stand in the flames of God until we become all fire, pure and blazing. The vow here is the traditional Benedictine vow of *conversio morum*, meaning conversion of one's ways, or conversion of life—not as one exalted moment, but as a continuous willingness to change, and grow, and move, to cooperate with the taking and giving which life brings, the Dark and Light faces of God. If we do not brace ourselves against such, but walk without reservation into the furnace, a whole new life opens before us. In an ancient text called *The Odes of Solomon*, the Christ descends into the fires of hell, and speaks the following words:

> *I have opened the gates that were bolted*
> *I have shattered the bars of iron*
> *and the iron has become red-hot;*
> *It has melted at my presence;*
> *and nothing more has been shut*
> *Because I am the gate for all beings.*
> *I went to free the prisoners; they belong to me*
> *And I abandon no one...*
> *I have sown my fruits in the hearts of mortals*
> *And I have changed them into myself...*

—Olivier Clement, *The Roots of Christian Mysticism*, New York: New City Press, 1995, pp.51-52.

Hospitality

The other side of such breaking down is mercy, compassion, and love. Expansive grace is always in tension with transforming fire. Here we take the vow of hospitality—a willingness to always be open and welcoming to others, to never finally shut the door on even the most difficult person (even if we have to apply a little tough love in the process!), and to always strive to see the best and highest in a person (the living flame of the Mystery burning in them) even when they are showing their worst face. This is how the saints, angels, and Divine powers approach us, and we can gradually learn to mirror them, by allowing them to act in us.

Humility

The veil has now been rent, and one finds the Indwelling Christ hidden at the core of one's being. We begin to hear the still small voice within—that speaks only truth. From this hidden place, the priest mediates the Divine Realities into the manifested world. The vow here is humility. Knowing our oneness with the Universal Logos—the Child of Light dancing at the edge of the Void—brings not pride, but humility. Humility is not a phony groveling before some angry god, but a gentle recognition of the truth beyond all egoic concern.

Stability

Passing through the Narrow Gate of humility, it becomes harder and harder to say anything meaningful in language. We only touch the hem of the realities of God, but our little efforts will continue to carry us forward. The primal form of our spiritual journey is our willingness to simply keep going, in the face of whatever may come. In the deepest, darkest night, we know the presence of the sustaining Mystery. The Divine is beyond light and darkness, and is revealed in both. Thus, we next vow stability—not stability in any organization or outer form, but stability on the spiritual Quest itself, following the winding way into the heart of the labyrinth of worlds, with abiding trust. I owe thanks to abbess and bishop Katherine Kurtz for this insight into stability.

Confidence

In balance with the primal form of the Quest is the primal force or energy of the Spirit, which can pour through us, taking with it all doubt, depression, and fear. These problems may continue to plague us on the level of the personality (and we may need to deal with them appropriately on that level), but we simultaneously come to know a deeper life, where it is always true (in the words of Liberal Catholic priest Paul Case) that "all power that ever was, is, or shall be, is here now!" Thus, we vow confidence in Spirit—a willingness to live from that place where God's energy infuses our life with vitality and direction, no matter what.

Obedience to God

Finally, we come to the integration of all things in the reunion with the Source of All, simple consciousness beyond all dualities. The vow is once again Obedience to God within and without—not in terms of following moral rules, but as naturally expressing the Divine Will through our conscious non-dual union with Spirit. Even here, we must remember that the Mystery is infinite, growth is infinite, and service is infinite. Even the deepest, highest state we can imagine is merely an open door to further growth and service. The sovereign is the servant of all.

If you wish to do so (and you should not do so lightly, as Life will test you afterwards, to see if you truly mean it), you may take a thread or cord, and knot it as you speak the vows outlined below. You could also string beads on a cord, or some other similar variant.

Knot the cord (or string the beads) as you speak the

vows, and then bind the cord around your body—wrist, ankle, or neck. I encourage you to speak the vows in the presence of a friend or spiritual advisor, as we tend to take more seriously what we say in front of others. They can hold us accountable! But you should do all the knotting and tying yourself—you freely take on these commitments. If you roll with the challenges Life brings you, you will have some interesting and wonderful opportunities for growth—at least I have had such, in working with this practice. But if you fight the experiences that come, it will be, well, interesting.....

The Taking of the Vows

In the presence of God and all the Holy Ones....

I vow my obedience to God, within and without, in all aspects of my life. (Tie a knot in the cord as you speak this, and each following vow.)

I vow that I will serve God, and all God's creatures, with a heart filled with joy, loving all creatures as God loves them, with thanksgiving.

I vow purity in heart and mind, that I may see with the Single Eye, and thus be a trustworthy guide to all who seek the Way.

I vow that I will never use violence, in thought, word, or deed, in the service of Christ. I will seek peace and follow after it, that the healing Spirit may renew the earth.

I vow that I will always regard all people, and all creatures, as my brothers and sisters in the Christ.

I vow poverty, in imitation of the Logos, poured out in the creation and renewal of the world. I will use whatever inner or outer treasures are given me, in service to the world, freely sacrificing myself but never presuming to sacrifice others.

I vow continuous conversion of my ways, that I may walk in the Way of Spirit, and open that Way to others.

I vow hospitality, welcoming the Divine Mystery in all people, without distinction, that I may serve that Glory living in them.

I vow humility and truth. May I bow before all as God's children, and thus come to know my true unity with the Spirit.

I vow stability on the Quest. May I be a Nameless Wanderer, never ceasing or turning aside on my journey into the Mystery.

I vow confidence in Spirit. May the joy and vitality of the Divine life fill my life. May love cast out all fear.

In the presence of God and all the Holy Ones, I reaffirm my vow of obedience to God, within and without, in all aspects of my life.

In token that I take these vows upon my soul freely, I bind this cord upon my own body. May the grace of the Mystery live in me, that I may be faithful. (Tie the cord around your wrist, ankle, or neck.)

CHAPTER FOUR:

Chapel & Equipment

A free priest of Christ needs no special place or equipment for her ministry. However, as the sacramental life delivers grace through the mediation of physical reality, it can be helpful to have a designated chapel or altar, and other equipment, if the circumstances of life allow.

The Chapel

If one has the space to separate an entire room for prayer, meditation, and sacramental work, it can be a great grace. A room which is repeatedly used only for sacred purposes gradually builds an inner atmosphere, which helps to carry the participants more quickly into consciousness of God. However, this is not often possible, and we have to improvise the best we can.

If one does have a room or part of a room to hand, the altar would traditionally be placed upon the eastern wall, the direction of the rising sun. Placement in the center or another direction is also possible, depending on individual insight. I have often worked with my altar in the north, a direction associated in western esotericism with the conjunction of the deep earth and the stars. If placement in the actual desired direction is not possible due to the room, one can simply designate the most convenient wall as "liturgical east (or whatever direction)." The inner pattern of the room will conform to your intention. Chapels can be as simple or as elaborate as you wish. You might have a lectern to hold the Gospels, icons on the wall, a presence lamp hung from the ceiling, and/or a triangle of tall candleholders marking a sanctuary space before the altar. A study of sacred architecture, from Quaker meetinghouses to Russian cathedrals, will provide ideas and patterns with which you can work.

Altar

A simple altar can be constructed on any surface—a table or dresser, for example. When living in a tiny room in New York City, I used a closet shelf. One can dedicate the space through prayers, sprinkling holy water, anointing with oil, perfuming with incense, or other such actions, as inspiration dictates. Minimally, you want to have a candle or oil lamp, and a cross or icon or other symbol indicating the altar's consecration to the Christian Mysteries. You can change the image from time to time, to indicate the season of the church year, or the particular aspect of the tradition with which you are currently working. For example, as I am focusing on Mary in my meditations, I have a hand-painted icon of Mary, by local iconographer Cassandra Stewart, over my altar at present. The icon arrived as a gift, which I took as a sign that I needed to work with the Blessed Mother. One can also surround the area with icons and statues of saints and angels (and photographs of departed friends and family) as invocations of their presence. If the surroundings and fire code allow, it is a good thing to keep a natural flame burning before the altar, as a sign of continual dedication and offering.

If you live in a space often visited by others who may not know about or understand your priestly work, you may have to find ways to accommodate that situation. In a previous apartment, I converted a small Buddhist cabinet altar for my purposes. When the doors are closed, it appears simply as a decorative wooden cabinet. A friend of mine created a larger, similar cabinet altar from a sizeable piece of furniture originally designed to hold a TV and stereo.

Altar Cloth

If a dedicated piece of furniture is not possible, one can create a blessed altar cloth or altar stone, which can be brought out as needed. A small altar cloth can be very useful for travel, as well. Orthodox priests use an antimension—a small cloth depicting Christ, containing one or more relics, and blessed and signed by a bishop. You don't need to follow all the Orthodox guidelines, but you could create a cloth, with an appropriate image drawn, painted, or embroidered upon it. You can sew into it (perhaps in a small pocket), one or more sacred items. This could be a relic of a saint, or a snippet of your grandmother's prayer-book, or a fragment of stone from a sacred site. If you meditate upon the spiritual foundations of your work as a priest, you will be led to the items you should place in the cloth (or alternately, within the stone, or under your physical altar). Even if you have a large altar, covered with elaborate paraments, this little cloth can rest beneath. When you serve in another location, or go on a trip, the cloth can be easily folded up and travel with you. Small, folding icons of Christ, Mary, or the saints, are also excellent for travel.

Vestments

Priestly vestments can be a wonderful for special occasions, but are by no means necessary. If one has the ability to sew, or the funds to buy them, they are nice to have, but if not, there is no loss. Beyond the actual wearing of vestments, some priests find it useful to visualize themselves in their vestments (even if they are really wearing blue jeans and a tee shirt) as a way of shifting consciousness prior to engaging in priestly work.

The main items of sacerdotal vesture are as follows:

The alb—This is a simple white robe. It is the baptismal garment of any Christian, and signifies purity in Christ and a share in the resurrection body. It also covers the more personal appearance of our secular clothing.

The stole—This is a long strip of cloth, which is draped diagonally over one shoulder for deacons, and around the neck for priests and bishops, over the alb. Most simply, it is the yoke of service in the priesthood, and the flow of God's energy moving through our bodies. If a priest owned no other vestments, it would be advisable to have at least a white stole.

The chasuble—A large, poncho-like outer garment, often worn over alb and stole by priests and bishops, generally only at the Eucharist. The stole and chasuble are usually in the seasonal liturgical color, or white, if the appropriate color is not available.

There are many other vestments—dalmatics for deacons, miters for bishops, and so on. The items above are primarily Roman and Anglican vestments, and one can complicate matters by considering the Orthodox equivalents. Beyond vestments, there are other related items such as the crosier (shepherd's staff) of a bishop and pectoral crosses, as well as non-liturgical garb such as cassocks and clerical shirts. The usefulness of any of this gear depends on one's setting, and one's personality. Some people will find them useful tools, while to others they will be highly artificial. A priest with a public liturgical ministry will have more use for an array of vestments than one with a hidden ministry of intercession.

As with varieties of vestments, there are many different color schemes in use for the church year. Some sacramental churches, including most of the Orthodox, do not use specific colors. But, for the sake of giving a simple guide, the following are fairly standard, as suggestions for colors for altar coverings and vestments:

White or Gold—Easter, Christmas, major festivals related to Christ, angels, saints (except apostles and martyrs)

Red—Pentecost, major festivals of the Holy Spirit, apostles, martyrs

Violet—seasons of penance and expectation—Advent and Lent

Green—all other times

A Sacred Relic

Even if one does not wear priestly garb, and does not exercise a public ministry, it can still be a very good thing to have some small item, such as a ring or necklace or cord, which one wears as a continual sign of one's ordination and dedication. It should be chosen carefully, cleansed with holy water, and then blessed. You might speak words over it, pass it through the altar flame, breathe upon it, and coat it with sacred oil. You could even place it in or under the chalice while celebrating the Eucharist. After blessing it in whatever way seems appropriate, you could leave it on the altar for a few hours or even days, asking the Spirit to continue the process of blessing the item, prior to wearing it. Interesting things can happen. Once when visiting someone in a jail, I noticed an attorney in the waiting room focusing her attention on a small silver ring I wear on my right hand. She looked up and said, "I know this is a bizarre question, but are you a priest?"

Chalice and Paten

The chalice and paten, or more simply, sacred cup and plate, are the primary implements of Eucharistic celebration. Any cup and plate can be used, but, if at all possible, it is helpful to have a specially consecrated set, reserved for the communion. Those familiar with western esotericism will recognize the paten as the implement of earth (recalling the earth of our bodies, and the body of Christ), and the chalice as the implement of water (the fluid of our blood, and the blood of Christ). A visit to a church supply store or a potter's booth at a craft fair will often lead to a reasonably priced set, perhaps marked with appropriate symbols. If you know a potter or metal-smith, you could have a set specially crafted, made with specific intention for your priestly work. Once acquired, the chalice and paten can be blessed, and signed with chrism in the shape of a cross. However, their true blessing comes through repeated use as vessels for the living mystery of the sacrament.

Over time, one will gather various additional implements for sacramental work—containers for water and wine, books of traditional liturgical materials for resource purposes, candles, an incense burner or oil diffuser, icons, statues, and so on. One may also want to keep a supply of blessed water and oil on hand.

Holy Water

To make holy water, you take a quantity of salt, and a bowl of water, separately. Over each, the priest prays that the substance be purified and blessed, and then combines the two by sprinkling the salt into the water in the shape of a cross, three times. If you have water from a sacred source (such as Lourdes or Glastonbury) you could add some to the holy water. Holy water can be used for baptism, and is very useful for blessing objects, people, and spaces, through sprinkling. A very traditional way of blessing a house is to draw a line of holy water across all entrances (doors, windows) and then sprinkle it through the rooms (perhaps accompanied by candles, incense, and spoken prayer).

Chrism

The word "Christ" means "the anointed one"—hence the centrally important use of oil in the sacraments. Blessed oil is traditionally made by a bishop on Holy Thursday (the Thursday prior to Easter, when we remember the Last Supper, and the origins of the Christian priesthood), but can certainly be created at other times of the year if need dictates. In the Eastern churches, there is usually only one blessed oil, called chrism. Chrism is traditionally a mixture of olive oil and aromatics (balsam, frankincense, myrrh, etc—recipes differ). Western churches tend to bless three oils—the oil of the catechumens (for use in baptism, and priest ordinations), the oil of the sick (for anointing the sick), and chrism (for confirmation and the consecration of bishops). One can create the three oils with elaborate ceremonial, but for most independent clergy, it is probably easier to just have a supply of chrism on hand. To make chrism, you blend the oil and aromatics while breathing over the mixture, and praying that it be infused with the power of the Spirit. Those who have an interest in the traditional qualities of certain plants and incenses can make use of that knowledge in their chrism recipe. Also, oil from sacred sources can be added. I often include some drops of oil from the memorial lamp of St John Maximovitch, and oil blessed with the relics of St Anne, in my chrism.

CHAPTER FIVE:

Cycles of Prayer

In the teaching of the Incarnation of Christ, we see Divinity in time, space, and history. The liturgical cycles are a way of expressing the sanctification of time in Christ, as well as continuing to renew our participation in the pattern of redemption revealed therein.

Daily

The first cycle is that of the day. Dawn turns to midday, which gives way to dusk, which deepens into midnight. Light and darkness, sun and moon, waking and sleeping play back and forth. Prayer, whether the breviary, the Mass, or some other form, punctuates the day, infusing it with grace. The most traditional times for prayer are the threshold points of morning (leading into light) and evening (leading into darkness). We may find alternate times, but there is great value in keeping a regular rhythm, even if other, additional practices come and go. Traditionally the liturgical day follows Jewish custom in running from sundown to sundown.

Weekly

The next rhythm is that of the week. Sunday is the day of the Resurrection, when we remember and participate in the renewal of all things. If the Eucharist is not celebrated on any other day during the week, it should be celebrated on Sunday. Thursday is also a day traditionally sacred to the Eucharist (as the day of the Last Supper), and another good time for mass. Wednesday (the day of the betrayal by Judas) and Friday (the day of the crucifixion) are days of fasting and penance. One need not follow any harsh ascetic practices, but it can be helpful to pause during the week for retrospection and simplification. Saturday has often been dedicated to Mary and the feminine mysteries in Christianity. If these attributions appeal, they can help to shape a rhythm of weekly prayer and ritual. Another, less well known weekly rhythm relates to the angels. The seven archangels before the throne of God are assigned to the days as follows: Sunday (Michael), Monday (Gabriel), Tuesday (Khamael), Wednesday (Raphael), Thursday (Tzadkiel), Friday (Haniel), and Saturday (Uriel). One might simply implore the angel of the day for intercession and protection. Or, if a more elaborate practice is desired, one can find such in bishop David Goddard's book, *The Sacred Magic of the Angels*. Goddard also has developed a series of sacramental blessings, given on the appropriate days of the week, which link the recipients more strongly to the seven archangels. In my own experience, these blessings or empowerments are highly effective.

The Cycle of the Year

Third, we have the rhythm of the church year, which encompasses three distinct cycles—the life of Christ, the sanctified cycle of the earth's own life, and the feasts of the saints. We can only give cursory treatment to these great rhythms here. Among the many helpful books for further exploration, I would particularly recommend *Patterns in Magical Christianity* by Nicholas Whitehead, *The Christian Year* by Evelyn Francis Capel, *The Time of the Spirit* by George Every, Richard Harries, and Kallistos Ware, and *Holidays and Holy Nights* by Christopher Hill.

First, the life of Christ (and to some extent, the life of Mary) is recapitulated annually through the liturgical year. We move through these patterns and stories again, as they become more deeply inscribed within our own lives. The expectation of the coming Messiah fills Advent with hope, which is fulfilled in the birth of Jesus at Christmas. The season following includes the extension of this hope to the Gentiles (in the persons of the Magi), the baptism of Christ by John, and the beginnings of the public ministry, all associated with Epiphany. In Lent, we feel the escalating tension of Jesus' encounter with political and religious authorities, and are pushed to ponder anew his question: "Who do you say that I am?" Holy Week begins on the high note of the triumphal entry into Jerusalem on Palm Sunday, and then descends through the last supper on Maundy Thursday to the crucifixion on Good Friday, and the entombed silence of Holy Saturday. Easter and the season which follows it bring us into the mysterious presence of the Risen One, who has to continually assure us: "Fear not." He leaves us at the Ascension, forty days after Easter, and sends the Holy Spirit upon us, ten days later at Pentecost. The remainder of the year is spent reflecting on how we can live out the Gospel in our lives, before the days darken and we find ourselves again in Advent, watching anew for the long expected one.

The story of Mary is interwoven with that of her son, and the feasts related to her conception, her birth, her death, and assumption into heaven, also punctuate the year. To give an example of how one might work with a season or feast in vision, here is one attempt to enter the mystery of the Assumption of Mary in vision:

Entering deeply into meditation, we find ourselves within a circular temple, open to the clear night sky above. In the center of the temple, set into the floor, is a large, round, dark mirror of obsidian, in which the circling stars are reflected. In the center of the mirror kneels a diminutive, ancient woman. Her long white hair falls over her robes and onto the mirror. Her aged fingers search the stellar patterns reflected before her, watching the movements of destiny.

Long ages ago, it was by such patterns that she found her way to help a young woman who was about to give birth to a Child whose origins lay far beyond the stars. We stand before Mary Salome, midwife to the birth of Christ, witness to his death and resurrection, companion to the Magdalene on her journeys.

As our company draws near, Salome rises with an ease which belies her years, and walks with bare feet to the edge of the mirror, to meet us. She takes our hands into her own, and we feel great warmth as she looks within our eyes, grinning gently with a toothy smile. She can read the patterns of our souls as easily as those of the stars. One can hide nothing from her gaze, but there is no need to fear.

From within her cloak, she pulls a gauzy red veil. The color is at first only slightly visible to us in the thin starlight, but grows unnaturally brighter, as the veil seems to take on a life of its own, whirling about our company. We feel the tight grip of Salome's gnarled hand, steadying our own, as the veil grows and whirls, brighter and brighter, encompassing us in brilliant red light.

As the movement stops, we look about us. We are in somewhat rustic and dusty stone house. The air blowing through the windows has a salty touch, probably from a nearby sea. Those gathered in the house seem sad and quiet. We follow their gaze to a couch, where we see the body of a beautiful woman, perhaps in her 40s or 50s. It is Mary of Nazareth.

Mary's body is completely covered by the thin veil of red gauze. Salome leads us forward to kneel before the couch. She touches Mary's arm with an almost motherly affection, rooted in years of companionship. As Salome turns to us, she smiles, and lifts the corner of the veil. The flashing starlight emanating from the body of Mary is so bright that we fall backwards, momentarily blinded. Salome returns the veil to its place, and still rubbing our eyes, we take our places among the gathered company, in silent prayer, around the body.

As night draws on, no one moves to light a lamp, as the glow of Mary's body through the veil fills the room with a soft red light. The peace of the moment grows so intense as to be almost unbearable to our scattered and divided souls. A gentle roaring seems to fill our ears, and we look up to see a triple flame of fire suspended over the body.

The flame grows, becoming a column of translucent divine fire, surrounding the couch upon which the Holy Mother rests. Within the fire, we sense more than see the presence of Michael the Archangel, who stands before the face of God. As the mighty archangel touches the Mother upon her forehead, she rises, brilliant and vibrantly alive, as if she had only been sleeping.

Enfolded within the blazing wings of the angel, Mary rises upward. It is as if the roof of the house no longer exists, and we can see the stars above, circling as if to make a crown. From her hands fall drops of brilliant star-fire, which settle on our foreheads and shoulders. As this blessing burns its way into our being, and Mary moves beyond sight, we hear her voice within our souls, telling us that we too shall rise, and all creation with us....

Salome picks up the red veil which had fallen to the floor. She wraps it around our shoulders in comfort. We close our eyes for a moment, and when we reopen them, we are back in the star temple, standing next to the mirror. Salome invites us to stay and watch the mirror with her, for awhile, before returning to the outer world, in our own time.

Here are a couple more examples of working with a feast day in vision:

Easter. *We find ourselves within a beautiful walled garden, at deepest midnight. Before us lies a new tomb, sealed with a large stone. It is guarded by soldiers, but they have fallen asleep, and lay slumped upon the ground. Mary Magdalene walks up behind us, and touches us on the shoulder. She leads us to the tomb, and with a gesture of profound love, she kneels before it as quiet tears stream down her face. We kneel with her.*

The earth begins to shake with a tremor, and we hear

stones cracking, as we are knocked backwards. Strangely, this earthquake is accompanied by a sense of profound peace, and a total lack of fear. The soldiers continue to sleep deeply, even as the ground trembles beneath them. As the stone rolls back from the tomb, we see the Christ, shining like the sun itself, rising up before us. Even in the midst of the blazing light, we see his face, gently smiling, and his wounds, fresh with dripping blood.

We reach toward him, and he raises his hand, not in prohibition but in a gesture of blessing. As his hand rises, the brilliant light streams outward in all directions. Our vision is momentarily overwhelmed, but as the intensity subsides, we see that the Christ is no longer before us. However, we are now profoundly aware of the light and fire of the resurrection burning deep within all substance, coursing in our own blood, shining from our eyes, blazing forth from the rocks and trees of the garden. The light breaks open all the frozen places within us, and within the planet, brining new life and vitality.

Closing our eyes in contemplation, we rest for a moment, and then look again to see that we are gazing upon an altar flame in an underground temple. The altar flame resonates with the fire burning in us. We can stay here with the Magdalene as long as we like, returning to waking consciousness in our own time.

Transfiguration. I invite you to lay aside all cares, and sink deep into meditation for a few moments, resting in God's presence....

It is early morning, and we are walking up the stony hill called Tabor with Jesus and some of his other disciples. In this moment, with the soft beginning of dawn on the eastern horizon, we are walking in quiet companionship.

At the top of the hill, Jesus, clad in a simple, seamless white garment, turns to face us. The sun has just risen above the horizon behind him, and at first we think we are seeing only the morning light. Something seems wrong with our vision—focus becomes difficult, and a rainbow spectrum of light plays before us. We look up, and our vision clears. Jesus stands before us, arms outstretched, shining with a clear white light, so bright that the sun dims behind him. Our legs give out beneath us, and we fall to the ground.

In vision, Moses the lawgiver and Elijah the prophet stand to either side of the Christ, speaking with him. Our impulsive friend Peter speaks out in praise of this moment, wanting to build three shrines on the spot. As Peter is speaking, a bright and shining cloud descends upon us all, and Peter is drowned out by a voice from beyond all time: "This is my beloved one, my Son. Hear him." Fear overtakes us, we shut our eyes, and tremble in God's presence. Then we feel a touch at our shoulder, and look to see Jesus giving his hand to lift us. "Arise, and have no fear. You are the light of the world. Let your light shine."

Finding the light of Christ within ourselves, we let it radiate brilliantly through us for a few moments, shining like the sun into the world...

The Seasons

In addition to the re-presentation of the lives of Jesus and Mary, the Christian tradition also sanctifies the natural cycle of the year. We are all familiar with the four seasons found in temperate climates, and marked by the two solstices (approximately June 21st and December 21st) and two equinoxes (approximately

March 21st and September 21st). Perhaps less familiar are the cross quarter days, which mark the mid-point between each solstice and equinox—approximately February 2nd, May 1st, August 2nd, November 1st. Like most of the world's religious traditions, Christian feasts have attached themselves to this cycle. According to some traditions, when the earth received the body of Christ at his burial, there was a radical joining of the two. Thus, the earth itself is revealed as the body of Christ and the rhythms of the life of the planet are made one with the rhythms of the Christian mystery.

The exact dates of the astronomical solstices, equinoxes, and cross-quarters vary slightly from year to year. For our purposes, this does not really matter, as they are tides which last for a time, rather than moments which must be exactly pin-pointed. March 25th is the Annunciation, when Jesus is conceived in the womb of Mary by the power of the Spirit, just as new life arises again in the spring. Easter often falls not too far from the spring equinox, also. June 24th is the Birth of John the Baptist. The connection of this feast to Midsummer may not be immediately apparent, but one can ponder the words of John: "I must decrease that he may increase." St John's birth sees the sun at its height in the northern hemisphere, from which it descends to its lowest at the winter solstice, near the birth of Christ at December 25th, when it begins to increase again. Between these two points, we find Michaelmas, on September 29th, a celebration of the angels, and especially of the fiery archangel Michael, whose flaming wings are perhaps reflected in the leaves of autumn.

Forty days after Christmas, we come to the cross

quarter day of Feb 2nd, usually known as Candlemas. We remember the dedication of the infant Jesus in the temple, and we bless the candles we will use in the coming year, just as light and warmth tentatively begin to reappear in nature. By the next cross quarter, May 1st, spring is in full bloom, and we celebrate the Virgin Mary, crowing her with flowers. In the modern Roman rite, May 1st is also sacred to her spouse, St Joseph the Worker. We also find the blessing of human work on August 1st, traditionally known as Lammas ("Loaf-Mass"), when loaves made from the new wheat were taken to church for blessing. This cross quarter may also be related to the Transfiguration on August 6th, when divinity shines forth through matter. The darkening days of November bring us to the final cross quarter, and the feasts of All Saints (November 1st) and All Souls (November 2nd), when we remember and strengthen our communion with the dead.

Here is a vision for working with Candlemas:

I invite you to lay aside all cares, and sink deep into meditation for a few moments, resting in God's presence....

We are standing in the shade of the stone wall of the Jerusalem temple, watching the scene that is unfolding before us. Old Simeon and Anna are walking toward a young couple who have come to present their child to God. Simeon and Anna have no position in the temple, and some of the priests think they are more than a little crazy. They are both very old, and hang around saying their prayers. They have been here as long as anyone remembers, and seem part of the furniture of the place.

As the young mother, holding her child, approached Simeon, we find ourselves inwardly remarking on a silent grace and strength which seems to surround this girl. Who is she? Simeon took the baby in his arms, and began to cry out, "O Lord, now I can die in peace! You have let me see your promised salvation! This child will be a light to the world!"

If we had not seen the bearing of the mother, we might think Simeon had finally lost his mind. But something of his wonder and respect rubs off on us, and we pause. Simeon turns to the mother, peers at her through his aged eyes, and says, "This child will be the fall and rising of many in Israel. A sign of contradiction. A sword will pierce your heart, and the thoughts of many hearts will be revealed." The mother does not speak a word, but her expression is a beauty formed of the perfect union of sorrow and joy, peacefully accepted.

Anna then takes the child, and her whole aged being lifts upward in the thanksgiving her lips utter. Who is this child, and what sorrowful joy has he brought upon us?

The following is an attempt to gain something of a living sense of the power of Christ in the earth, through a vision, taking St. Mary Salome as a guide, once again:

We find ourselves again within the circular star temple, open to the clear night sky above. Upon the dark mirror in the center of the temple kneels Mary Salome. Her long white hair falls over her robes and onto the mirror. She gazes into the mirror with deep intensity. As we draw near, we see Orion with his bright belt of stars, and Taurus the bull, both above us in the sky, and reflected in the mirror. Salome greets us with warmth and a twinkle of humor in her eyes. From within the folds of her cloak, she draws a yellow veil, that shines in the darkness as if woven from golden sunlight.

Salome is far more agile than we would expect from her

great age, and she begins a slow dance, moving around us with the golden veil. Then, standing in the center of the mirror, she begins to spin faster and faster, with the veil about her, until it is as if there was a spinning sun of golden light in the center of our circle. The intense vibration of the dance produces a mystical music, and we find ourselves transfixed by the brilliant light and the glorious sound.

Within the golden light, we begin to see the outlines of a figure moving. At first we think Salome must be slowing her dance, but if anything, the movement and sound have intensified. It is a beautiful young man with golden hair, clad in a cloak of stars, dancing to the rhythm of the music of the spheres. Or perhaps his dance sets that rhythm… He turns to us and smiles. As he spreads his arms, and his cloak opens, we see his heart exposed, as a living sun within the sun. We feel the loving radiance which flows out to us…

The image shifts again, and now we see the earth, spinning amidst its cloak of stars, gently bathed in the golden light of the sun. As we watch the dance of our planet, the voice of the young man speaks to us: "I am he who groans within all creation until that perfect day. I am he who is already risen in the heart of all things. The rhythm of my dance grows stronger in the movement of the earth, and in the beating of your heart. Listen and follow my steps."

It is as if the words of this most wise Fool have rent a veil before our heart of hearts. It is as if our very chests have been ripped open, and the golden radiance recedes in the light of a white sun which spins and sings within us…..

As the light dims, we find that we stand again with Salome within the star temple. The ancient priestess comes to each of us, and with a wink, gently ties a golden thread from her veil around one of our fingers. Night is dark about us, and the constellation of the great bull is still reflected in the mirror. We stay with her and watch, rubbing our fingers against the thread, until we are ready to return to outer awareness.

Angels' and Saints' Days

In addition to the lives of Christ and Mary and the cycles of the earth, the tradition also celebrates festivals of saints and angels scattered throughout the year. Saints are often celebrated on the day of their physical death, when they were "born into eternity." Or perhaps the feast day remembers their birth, or a miracle, or some other defining moment. Angelic feast days may relate to natural cycles, or to the larger church year. For example, the traditional feast of the Archangel Gabriel is March 24th, the day before the Annunciation, when Gabriel's message to Mary is commemorated.

One can deepen contact with the angels through visionary meditation, such as this working with the Archangel Michael:

Sinking deeply into meditation, we awaken in inner vision to find ourselves kneeling in a bare chapel, before a large stone altar. Burning on the altar is a single flame encased in red glass. Above and behind the altar hangs a great spear, lined with dried blood. The words of a childhood prayer run in our heads: "Holy Michael Archangel, defend us in battle. Be our protection against the malice and snares of the enemy...."

A sense of pressure begins to build in our heads, and our vision seems strange. The red light on the altar grows and pulses, and becomes a brilliant column of red, orange, and golden light, the presence of the mighty archangel who burns as a flame before the throne of God. We initially feel fear, but the emotion transforms as our bodies are flooded with strength and energy, and a profound uprightness.

Within the column of fire, we begin to detect the outlines of a winged and muscular warrior. He reaches behind him and grabs the spear from the wall, which becomes as a lance of light in his hand. Michael looks at us in silence. In the depth of his gaze, we fall beyond the confines of time and space. At our core, we feel the question which is the very meaning of his name: Who is like God?

Suddenly, we are pulled from our contemplation, as we realize that the archangel has plunged a lance of light into each of us. The lance joins with our spine, transfixing us. We feel it within as a rod of power, but not our personal power…. This is an axis of the Divine will, around which all the elements of our lives can organize in balance and service. Transfixed by the lance of the archangel, we need have no fear of any foe, within or without.

We rest in the protection found in total vulnerability to the will of God. Looking up, we see only the small red flame upon the altar. In our own time, we return to outer awareness.

If you are unfamiliar with the saints, there are many books which give a calendar of festivals, with readings and information. A good example, with a saint for each day, is Robert Ellsberg's excellent book, *All Saints*. Over time, you may build up your own calendar of saints and angels who hold particular significance for you. In addition to learning about a given saint, you can also work with the patterns of the saint's life in ritual, or in vision. You can begin with material from the legends of the saint, or just open to the being, and see where you are led. The following is an attempt to do so with St John the Apostle:

Falling into deep meditation, we find ourselves on a rocky, sun-drenched island. A strong ram goes ambling by, over the rocks, and we follow him, up and down. Finally, coming over the top of a little rise, we see the ram standing by an old man of regal bearing, but wearing tattered clothes, next to a rough stone tower. The old man is petting the ram, and feeding him bits of things. They are clearly friends.

The old man invites us into the tower, and we sit down with him at a table on the ground level, where we can talk with him about whatever we wish. After finishing our discussion, we follow him up a spiral stair to the upper level of the tower, which is a chapel with a simple stone altar. A chalice rests upon it, filled with wine.

The priest-king hands us a flaming sword, and instructs us to insert it through the center of the top of the altar. We do so, and it slides in easily, nearly up to the hilt. As the sword joins with the altar, the whole altar begins to flame with the fire of the sword. Even the lip of the chalice is ringed with divine fire. And the old man's ragged clothes have become transformed into a beautiful vestment of living fire. Everything is burning but nothing is consumed.

As the priest-king raises the chalice, a bolt of light and fire descends upon the tower, and all visual awareness merges into the lightning.... As vision slowly returns, the priest-king is holding the flaming chalice at the level his forehead. A white serpent rises out of it, and coils itself around his head, forming a crown.

He summons us forward, and gives us to drink from the chalice. The fire does not burn, but rather warms our bodies, even on the physical level. The priest-king, St John, says to each of us: "Stand in the fire, not flinching, and feel the life of Christ awakening in you." As we drink, visionary awareness again dissolves into undifferentiated brilliance, and as we regain awareness, we find ourselves back where we began.

And again with St. Peter: *We find ourselves again within the circular star temple, open to the clear night sky above. Upon the dark mirror in the center of the temple kneels Mary Salome. Her long white hair falls over her robes and onto the mirror. Her aged fingers search the stellar patterns reflected before her, continuing to feel their way across the obsidian surface, as she looks up to notice our approach. She rises to meet us, clasping our hands one by one. Salome looks deep within our eyes, with an infinite compassion, as she once looked into the shining eyes of a newborn Child, with love deepened by the suffering she knew was held within his destiny.*

She returns to kneel upon the mirror, and we kneel in a circle around her. From within the folds of her cloak, she draws a blue veil. We know we are not seeing with ordinary vision, as the color is bright even in the faint starlight. She smoothes the veil gently over the mirror, with the care with which one might cover a sleeping child, or a newly dead loved one. The ancient woman begins to softly moan, and her voice rises and falls in mourning cries which pierce us to the heart. We feel a cosmic sorrow that engulfs our being, cracking us through and through. Yet somewhere in the bottomless pit of this sorrow is a joy that is not separable from it. . . .

As Mary Salome continues to chant, the veil upon the mirror swirls and ripples, and we look up to see that we are sitting around a small pool under a darkening sky. The pool is surrounded by olive trees, and fed by a gentle stream flowing down from a hill. As our eyes follow the stream up the hill, they meet a gruesome vision. A crude wooden cross is planted in the earth, with a man crucified upside down upon it. He appears near death, with blood and sweat pouring from him, and yet his face conveys a profound serenity.

Salome speaks to us: "Silver and gold had he none, but what he had, he has given." We realize this is Peter, prince of apostles, the impetuous one, now in full alignment with the shepherd who gives his life for the sheep. He looks upon us with great peace, and as the last of his life slips from his body, we pause to ponder the scene before us.... (short pause)

Looking into the pond, we see a dark ripple where blood flowing from Peter's body into the stream above has trickled down into the pool, and now dances amidst the first reflected twinkles of the evening stars.

Salome reaches into her pool, her hand dripping with blood and water. She comes to each of us, and places her hand gently upon our forehead. As we feel the fluid running down our faces, we close our eyes and enter a deep silence....

(long pause)

As we open our eyes again, we are back within the star temple, where we began. Salome dries our faces a bit with the blue veil, and invites us to stay as long as we like, before returning to outer awareness.

CHAPTER SIX:

Training

Priesthood training is a very contested topic within the independent sacramental movement. Some provide virtually no training (adopting the sink or swim method) while others insist on years of seminary. As usual, the balance lies in the middle. To my mind, the one indispensable aspect of training is spiritual formation. If a would-be priest has a regular spiritual practice, and a degree of genuine realization of the mysteries she will celebrate, she can fill in the gaps of historical and theological background as time allows. She will also achieve competency in sacramental work through doing it—which is the only effective way to learn liturgy. The apostles were sent out bearing the power of the Spirit, not academic credentials. A person with great theological learning, but a shallow spiritual life, will make an exceeding poor (and probably dangerous) priest.

We have treated spiritual life and sacramental practice in separate chapters. While other aspects of training are of lesser importance, these matters should not be ignored, and can enrich the life and work of any priest. Thus, we will consider the study of theology, ethics, church history, scripture, and pastoral care, for the free priest.

Theology

The meaning of the word "theology" is "knowledge of God." True theology is the knowledge of God which is given to us in prayer and meditation. We then reflect on that experience, and upon what we receive of the Christian community's experience though tradition and scripture. We can also ponder what we know from other sources, and from other traditions, as all truth is of God. While the mind can definitely be the "slayer of the Real," it also can be sanctified as a microcosmic reflection of the Divine Logos.

The wise priest will make time to read widely in theology from multiple traditions within Christianity. Some theologians are very traditional, while others are boldly re-thinking inherited doctrines. Some are systematic in approach, while others take a more ad hoc, topical approach. Fiction (e.g., Sue Monk Kidd, *The Secret Life of Bees*) and poetry (e.g., Marie Howe, *The Good Thief*) can also become vehicles of theology. All are worth reading. Even if you vehemently disagree with an author, the internal conversation which is stimulated will likely lead to new insights. If one is unfamiliar with theology, the easiest way to start is a journey to a well-stocked local bookstore, especially a university bookstore, or a library. You can simply scan the theology shelves for books which strike your interest. These books will, in turn, provide further references to follow. You might begin with a broad-ranging systematic theology (*Systematic Theology* by James William McClendon), a collection of occasional essays (*The Hauerwas Reader* by Stanley Hauerwas), an examination of a particular doctrine (*God For Us: The Trinity and Christian Life* by Catherine LaCugna), an aspect of life (*Violence Unveiled* by Gil Baillie), or an exercise in "theology from the margins" (*Our Tribe: Queer Folks, God, Jesus, and the Bible* by Nancy Wilson).

After tasting something of the theological tradition as it is practiced today, you then need to engage in your own theological reflection. Who or what is God? Who is Jesus? What is it to be a human being? How do we understand religious experience? When pondering these questions, philosophical reflection and research are helpful, but one should also contemplate. Lighting a candle and invoking Christ, you can simply go within and find the light at the natural center of gravity of the body (the general area of the solar plexus and belly button). Sinking into the light, and asking the wisdom of Christ to suffuse you, you can let your questions go to the Divine, and see what insight may follow, whether immediately or over time.

We can also join the apostles in vision, asking, "Who is our strange friend, Jesus?"

MEDITATIONS

I invite you to lay aside all cares, and sink deep into meditation for a few moments, resting in God's presence....

We are together with our friends, on a small boat, crossing the Galilee's lake. Night is coming on, and the gentle waves rock our boat. It is a lake we know well, as many of us fished here for a living, before joining the company of Jesus. The stars slip gently behind some oncoming clouds.

Jesus is sleeping, curled up with a pillow. The crowds have not given him any peace for days, and he is taking advantage of these brief moments, in trusted company, as we cross the lake. The wind begins to pick up, and we look at one another in apprehension, as we know well how quickly squalls can blow up.

Before long, the waves are growing higher, lightning is flashing, the wind is whipping, and our little boat is quickly being swamped. We are all desperately scrambling to bail water, and keep the boat upright in the raging sea. Still Jesus sleeps. One of us—incredulous that he could still be asleep—wakes him. "Save us, Master! We are surely going to drown!"

Jesus rises to stand in the midst of the tossing boat, with a poise and balance that immediately brings a sense of control to our frantic situation. He asks, "Why are you afraid? Where is your faith?" Jesus raises his arms, and addresses the wind and the sea, firmly and clearly. At once, the storm begins to calm, the clouds roll by, and we once more see the stars shining peacefully above us.

Jesus returns to his pillow, but our wonderment will allow no rest. We ask one another, "Who is our strange friend, that even the elements obey him?"

Ethics

This is closely tied to theology, and as an area of study has often been called "moral theology." Our theological understanding is enacted in our form of life, but our form of life also conditions and makes possible our theological understanding. Ludwig Wittgenstein is well known for his remark that the gospels could mean something to him only if he lived completely differently. (*Culture and Value*, 33e) Only such a changed life can contain the mystery of the Christ.

We often react against ethics, due to the images of rigid parental figures about to rap us on the knuckles, or damn us to hell, for some infraction, probably having to do with sex. Such a narrow, rule-based approach is not really helpful. Picking up on the work of the narrative school of theology, I think it is more helpful to see ethics as the study of the saints. It is in the lives of the saints, official or not, that we see the virtues, the capacities formed in us by Christ, on display in the world. We may consider famous sanctified people of past ages (St Benedict, St Francis, Mother Ann Lee), or our own time (Dorothy Day, Thomas Merton, Henri Nouwen), or hidden, unknown souls among our own family and friends.

When learning an art, like baking bread or painting, there are many subtle aspects which are only picked up by working alongside someone who already knows the ropes. These elements cannot always be easily reduced to written principles. Living a transformed life in Christ is similar. There is much that can be gathered by journeying, in life, thought, and/or vision, alongside those who have, to some degree, mastered the Way. Even if we might choose differently from these spiritual friends and ancestors, their lives challenge us to find ways to respond to God's call, and enlarge our own horizons.

For a start, you might pick out biographies of men and women from the tradition who appeal to you, or the collections of wisdom tales about the Desert Fathers or Mother Ann Lee and the early Shaker Elders. You can use the same meditation method we have used with biblical episodes, to enter into the saint's life in imaginal vision. Such vision can function as invocation, and you may find yourself in living contact with the saint. Through sharing in the energy of the saint's transformed existence, you may begin to know what ethics truly amounts to, and how your own life and activity need to change, in order to truly understand the Gospel.

I invite you to lay aside all cares, and sink deep into meditation for a few moments, resting in God's presence....

We are gathered with Jesus and some of his disciples, sitting outdoors in the hot sun. Children play around us, as people gather, talking to Jesus, challenging him, requesting his blessing.... We listen carefully to his voice, as all his words seem as much for us, as for the inquirers.

A young man in fine clothes approaches the Christ. We see a true reverence in his bearing. He asks with earnestness, "Good Teacher, what must I do to be saved?" Jesus proceeds to recount the commandments given to the people of Israel. The man replies, "But I have kept all these precepts from my youth." We feel within ourselves his frustration. How could all this goodness, all this religious observance, still leave a shadow upon the heart?

Jesus looks at the young man with such deep compassion

*and love that all of us feel it. We are all one in our vulner-
ability before such love. Extending his hands to the man,
Jesus speaks, "You lack only one thing. Sell what you have
and give to the poor. Let your treasure be in heaven. Come,
follow me."*

*The young man's face falls, and he walks away. Jesus
turns to us and says, "How hard it is for those with riches to
enter the kingdom of God. It is easier for a camel to pass
through the eye of a needle." Knowing our own clinging, to
possessions both inner and outer, we ask, "Who then can be
saved?" Jesus replies, "With God, all things are possible."*

*We feel the presence of Christ with us, giving hope in the
possibility of all things. We ponder within ourselves all those
things which prevent us from passing through the eye of the
needle….*

Church History

Obviously, both theology and the lives of God's holy ones take place in the context of time, which brings us to the history of the Church. This history is not something separate from us, but the story of the inner transmission which has come to rest on our shoulders. I have heard many new bishops speak of the sensation of something very weighty tangibly descending on them, carried by the hands of all the saints and sinners through whom it has been passed over the centuries. In order to understand what we have inherited, both the good and the bad (which, as with all human life, are often thoroughly mixed together), we must know something of this story.

The outer elements of the story are the people and institutions who have been the face of the Christian tradition for the last 2000 years. There are many standard histories easily available in any library or bookstore. While one may want to pursue histories of elements like Gnosticism, which were excluded from what became the mainstream, it is also very important to understand the central line of the tradition. It may have been forged by power and politics, but it is what has endured, and like it or not, one had best know what it is, and where it came from. Beyond the political/social/institutional history, there is also the history of thought (not just theology) within the tradition. There are a number of excellent histories of Christian thought, including those by William Placher and Jaroslav Pelikan. Finally, there is the story of how the Spirit moves and breathes through this often troubled history. This last story is the most difficult to tell, as it requires a deeper level of discernment. One of the most successful efforts remains Charles Williams' *The Descent of the Dove: A Short History of the Holy Spirit in the Church*.

We try to catch something of the original animating Spirit, which can then be traced through the by-ways of the history of the Christian community:

In addition to the larger scope of church history, any free priest would be well advised to acquire familiarity with the history of the independent sacramental movement. Most people who encounter an independent priestly ministry will be quick to ask about its historical background, and often its ordination lineage. At the risk of shameless self-promotion, I recommend the history chapter in my book, *The Many Paths of the Independent Sacramental Movement*, as a reasonably concise summary, with ample references for further exploration.

MEDITATIONS

I invite you to lay aside all cares, and sink deep into meditation for a few moments, resting in God's presence....

It is very early morning, and we are with our friend Mary Magdalene in the garden where Jesus has been buried. Mary came here in the dark before dawn, and found the tomb empty. She ran back to tell us all, and we followed her to the garden.

Mary is now leaning against a rock, in the faint light, weeping gently. Our own grief gnaws at us, and we are embarrassed at our emotions, and those of our friends. The stone which had covered the entrance to the tomb had been rolled back. Mary rises and goes to look again into the tomb, and we look over her shoulders into the cold stone chamber.

At first we think that the morning light is playing a trick with our tear-stained vision, but wiping our eyes, we see two creatures of pure light, like living stars, sitting within the tomb. They speak to Mary: "Woman, why are you weeping?" She replies, "They have taken my Lord." Before the angels have a chance to answer, we sense that someone is behind us, and we all turn, fearing it could be a soldier or some other hostile person.

Mary sighs, "It is just the gardener. Sir, do you know where they have taken Jesus?" The man speaks, "Mary", and we suddenly know it is Jesus. We feel him speaking each of our names, within us, in pure recognition.

Our tears are now tears of joy, and Mary reaches out to touch Jesus. He holds up his hand to stop her, saying, "Do not hold me, for I have not ascended to the Father. But go to my friends, and tell them I am ascending to my Father and your Father, my God and your God."

With that, Jesus vanishes just as quickly as he appeared. We stay by the empty tomb in the garden with Mary Magdalene for a few moments, knowing we will never be the same again…

Scripture

It is the rare Christian who reaches maturity without some level of scarring from scripture. This is no fault of scripture, but can be laid at the door of its interpreters, and their cultural enforcers. From our point of view, we can embrace scripture as a fascinating, often inspiring, and sometimes troubling account of one people's struggle to discover and relate to the Divine. When we step back from the oft touted belief that scripture is literally true and inerrant, presenting to us a fully accurate picture of God, we can breathe a huge sigh of relief. While parts of the Bible are among the most profound products of the human spirit, other parts describe a God we would not want as a next door neighbor, much less as the sovereign of the Universe. This quality of the Bible should not negate its value, but actually bring it closer to us. We know all too well the mixed and shifting character of our own insight into God's revealing grace. Why should that of our ancestors somehow be more perfect?

I am inclined to the idea (which I first learned from my Shaker friends) of open revelation. God's revelation did not stop around the year 100, but continues in full force at this present moment. As the Liberal Catholic priest Paul Case said, "All the power that ever was, is, or shall be, is here, now!" The Bible may be privileged as it recounts the origins (historical and legendary) of our tradition, but it is not unique, or infallible in any way. We can thus freely reach outside the canon to ancient documents (*The Gospel of St Thomas*), later high points of tradition (*The Little Flowers of St Francis*, or *The Rule of St Benedict*), and revelatory work closer to our own times (*The Book of Activity* of Fr Paul Blighton), to find the Word of God being spoken to us.

When we consider the Bible, or any other revelation, we can look at it from many different angles. First of all, it is wise to have an awareness of the outcome of historical and literary scholarship applied to the texts. The footnotes of many Bibles will provide basic information, as will widely available study guides and more advanced works of scholarship. We can learn a lot about when, how, and for whom the Biblical texts were written, and how they were shaped into the current canon. Besides its inherent interest, such study can go a long way towards dismantling any fundamentalism which may be lurking in us. We only err if we start to believe that historical-critical scholarship exhausts the meaning of scripture, or dictates the ways in which our communities may choose to use the text.

Following on from the literal/historical sense, we can also consider the possible allegorical and typological meanings of a passage, and how it may echo and foreshadow other parts of scripture. We can then move on to what has often been called "the moral sense," indicating not commandments of morality but the way in which the passage speaks directly to us in our present situation. In this regard, I have been helped by a little series of questions which came to me from Rev. Jim Rule and the Entheos Community, in Atlanta, Georgia:

> In this group we are not as interested in finding the "right" interpretation as we are in engaging with scripture deeply enough that we bump into this Jesus who will guide us as we need to go. Rather than repeating what most of us have done

before—discuss content and plot, context and culture, theology and morality—our discussion centers around the following questions:

What strikes me, grabs my attention first, about this passage?

What do I feel when I read it?

What "triggers" are set off in me by this passage?

If I were to argue back with this passage, what would I say?

Who do I identify with most/least in this reading?

What part of the audience am I? Is this passage directed at me?

If this were a story about parts of myself, if every part of the reading referred to an aspect of myself, how might that change my understanding of the reading?

My understanding of myself?

Finally, you might be drawn into the inmost, mystical meaning of a passage of scripture, which carries you into the depths of God. This may not be rational or articulable, but is nonetheless profoundly real. You might work with it in vision, entering the scene (whether the encounters of Jesus with various seekers, or the weighty visions of Ezekiel) and seeing where it takes you. If you are hearing the passage read or chanted, the rhythm of the words alone may carry you, especially when a powerfully poetic translation is used.

These methods, and many others you may discover, can provide resources for approaching the foundational texts of our tradition, in such a way that they lead us to the Divine, rather than constricting our experience.

Following is a meditation for working with the power of the Word in scripture:

I invite you to lay aside all cares, and sink deep into meditation for a few moments, resting in God's presence....

We are in a room deep within the temple complex. The walls stretch high above us, and we feel the cool stones beneath us. It is day, but the windows are small, and smoky lamps give additional light. We are sitting in a gathering of religious scholars, elderly men who have devoted their lives to plumbing the depths of God's revelation to Israel. Their fingers search their way across the crumbling scrolls.

We look up to see a young boy standing at the entrance to the room, his eyes sparkling with light from the high windows. One of the old men asks, "Son, are you lost?" The boy replies in calm assurance, "I am in my Father's house." The young Jesus walks into the center of our gathering. Isaiah's words flash across our minds, "...and a little child shall lead them..."

The boy begins to speak, drawing aside the veil of our minds, and revealing the mysteries of the living Word. Tears of awe and joy shine in the eyes of the scholars. We listen with all our being for what the Child has to say to us. We let his words reach deep within our minds and hearts, and rest in that depth for a few moments....

Pastoral Care

Each priest is always engaged in continuous learning, in response to what life brings to his or her doorstep. The Baptist radical Will Campbell likes to say that you do not have to seek for your ministry—it is always whatever is right under your nose. The same could be said for your training in the mysteries. The next avenues for learning always appear, if one is watching carefully. The last area we will consider in this chapter is pastoral care.

Pastoral availability to others is a duty of a priest. In a consecration liturgy written by bishop Tim Harris, the consecrator asks the new bishop and teacher, "Do you vow that you will never close the door on anyone, for in Christ Jesus, forgiveness is offered to all?" I can attest that it is a soul-rattling experience to be on the receiving end of that question, and I often ponder it when weighing a course of action.

A priest is not a psychologist or psychotherapist, and should not play at being such, unless she or he also has professional training in that field. It is very helpful for a priest to have familiarity with basic psychology, at least enough to know when matters require referral to a professional. There are also many fine works on pastoral counseling (*Theology and Pastoral Counseling* by Deborah Van Deusen Hunsinger) and spiritual direction (*Soul Friend* by Kenneth Leech). Beyond confession or sacramental consultation, the priest should limit her counseling and spiritual direction according to her training and skills. In any instance, the duty of the priest is to mediate the living presence of Christ in both seen and unseen ways, and convey his or her experience of the wisdom of the Christian tradition. This is a different role from that of a therapist or social worker, and should not be confused.

We can learn from the examples of pastoral care in tradition:

I invite you to lay aside all cares, and sink deep into meditation for a few moments, resting in God's presence....

We are seated around our teacher Ananias. We come here to his old ramshackle house in Damascus, to learn about Jesus. Ananias is deep in meditation, and the lines in his old face go limp in the flickering lamplight. He speaks falteringly, "The Lord Jesus is here.... He wants me to go to Judas' house on the straight street, to find Saul of Tarsus..." There is a long pause, and we wonder what is happening, as we know this Saul represents the religious authorities and hates our little community.

Ananias speaks again: "My dear ones, whom I love so much, we need have no fear. The Lord tells me that this Saul the persecutor will spread his name among the Gentiles and in Israel." Without a second's delay, Ananias rose and headed out of his house to the straight street. Half wondering if our teacher has finally gone insane, we follow, a few steps behind.

When we get to Judas' house, we find Saul there, sure enough, blind and in pain. He tells Ananais how Jesus appeared to him as in a flash of lightning as he was on his way to persecute our community in Damascus. He was knocked from his horse by the vision, and became blind.

Ananais, who had known Jesus and looked deeply in his eyes, laid his knotted old hands on Saul's balding head, and prayed in deep silence. He spoke, "Brother Saul, the Lord Jesus who appeared to you has sent me that you may regain

your sight, and be filled even now with the Holy Spirit."
Again, Saul was knocked to the ground and scales fell from
his eyes. . . . Before even leaving the house, Saul was baptized
by Ananias, giving him the new name Paul. Ananias also
fed him.

As we walk with Paul back to Ananias' house, where he
will stay with us for some time, we wonder at God's
grace. . . .

Learning to be a priest never ends. God is infinite,
and thus growth into the Divine Mysteries is infinite.
With these small suggestions, we can begin placing one
foot before other along this way.

CHAPTER SEVEN:

Conclusion

In parting, here is a homily I preached a couple of years ago, on the First Sunday of Advent, November 30, 2003:

In the late autumn, in our hemisphere, life draws inward. Days grow shorter and colder, leaves wither and fall, animals store food and find places to hibernate. The earth herself enters a time of quiet contemplation. Advent is the church's invitation to do likewise. We take a deep breath, and hold it for moment, watching for the coming of Christ.

During Advent, we watch for the birth of Jesus from Mary, and for the final coming of Christ in the consummation of all things. We also watch for how Christ comes to us, and among us, today.

Today's gospel recalls the potent image of the Son of Man coming in a cloud. The elders and eldresses of the Shaker community were fond of this passage. They interpreted it in an unusual way, which may not stand up to strict biblical interpretation, but nonetheless displays a profound spiritual insight.

The Shakers taught that the cloud in which Christ

comes is not some supernatural meteorological phe-
nomenon. Rather, it is the "cloud of witnesses," spoken
of in the *Letter to the Hebrews*. Christ comes in the cloud
of those gathered in the new life he brings.

For many of us, the "cloud of witnesses" may bring
to mind the great saints and martyrs, and seem far
removed from our more fragile and fallible reality. But
this is a mistake. As we ponder the meaning of the
cloud of witnesses in which Christ comes, we may be
helped by a story about the American Sufi teacher, Sam
Lewis.

Sam was not a Christian, but he was a great friend of
Jesus, and was once the spiritual director of a Christian
religious order. He taught in San Francisco from the
1960s until his death in 1971, at the age of 75. Sam was
best known for taking the students that everyone else
rejected. It did not matter if you were gay, if you had a
wild past, if you were running from the law, still struggling with drugs, homeless and dirty, whatever…. Sam
took you in, loved you, and cooked you dinner. If you
hung around, he might take a rest in his green kitchen
chair, and offer a little wisdom, as well.

One day, Sam and a rather motley crew of students
were at San Francisco airport, to meet someone. A
respectable businessman, shocked by this colorful
parade, muttered, "Who is that?!" Sam heard him,
turned and said, smiling, "This is the New Age, in person!"

After Sam died, some of his lectures on the New
Testament were published. A very insightful editor
chose "This is the New Age, in Person" as the title, as
that is surely the claim made for Jesus and his own dis-

reputable band of disciples, and for the community in which Jesus still lives today.

We are a tiny and, by mainstream standards, rather odd little community. Nonetheless, along with all others who gather to follow Jesus…. We are that cloud of witnesses in which he comes to the world today. We are the New Age, in person. We are the Kingdom, the God Movement, come upon the earth. Let us take time away from the holiday bustle, to watch for how this magnificent reality is manifesting in our lives.

Sam Lewis welcomed the misfits and oddballs of the world, and with great love, set a table before them. Today, Sam's friend, Jesus, known for eating with tax collectors and prostitutes, does the same for us. All are welcome to share this bread, this cup, in which we taste the ever new presence of the One who draws us here.

So let us prepare to feast with him.